"Margot Fedoruk plunges the reader into island life: love, sex, marriage, children, community, ferries, food, and the ocean itself. Intimate and funny, her story is also a testament to the vast amount of work women do, including the (unpaid) emotional and domestic. It will build your appetite—and fortunately the recipes are first-rate."

KATHY PAGE Rogers Writers' Trust Fiction Prize–winning author of *Dear Evelyn*

"By turns hilarious and heartbreaking, a timid girl from Winnipeg's North End becomes a boisterous, eloquent west coaster. Margot Fedoruk inherits fiercely resilient genes from her Big and Little Babas. Read on to discover how an unstoppable zest for living transformed a haphazard upbringing. And for her drool-worthy recipes!"

CAROLINE WOODWARD bestselling author of *Light Years: Memoir of a Modern Lighthouse Keeper*

"Margot Fedoruk asks herself: 'Is this a normal way to live? Would I choose this life again?' And you can't help but read on, waiting for the answer."

JACK KNOX humourist and bestselling author of *Fortune Knox Once: More Musings from the Edge*

"In Margot Fedoruk's exquisite memoir, longing hangs in the air like an unidentified fragrance—longing for an intact family, longing for the perfect love. When she finally achieves some version of both, you will want to cheer her on. And you'll want to taste-test the tantalizing recipes she offers along the way, too."

FRANK MOHER award-winning playwright, journalist, and media critic

"These are stories of hard separations and cold beers, of surviving the choices we make, and of forging home on a small island in the Pacific Northwest 'surrounded by green so dark that it soaked up the sun.' And the recipes? Shared like secrets between the closest of friends after just enough wine and just the right shade of twilight."

AMBER MCMILLAN author of *The Woods: A Year on Protection Island*

COOKING TIPS
FOR
DESPERATE
FISHWIVES

AN ISLAND
MEMOIR

MARGOT FEDORUK

Heritage House Publishing Company, Ltd.
heritagehouse.ca

*Cataloging information available from
Library and Archives Canada*

978-1-77203-395-3 (paperback)
978-1-77203-396-0 (e-book)

Edited by Paula Marchese
Cover and interior design by Setareh Ashrafologhalai
Cover illustration by Setareh Ashrafologhalai

The interior of this book was produced on
100% post-consumer recycled paper, processed
chlorine free, and printed with vegetable-based inks.

Heritage House gratefully acknowledges that the land on which we
live and work is within the traditional territories of the Lkwungen
(Esquimalt and Songhees), Malahat, Pacheedaht, Scia'new, T'Sou-ke,
and WSÁNEĆ (Pauquachin, Tsartlip, Tsawout, Tseycum) Peoples.

We acknowledge the financial support of the Government of
Canada through the Canada Book Fund (CBF) and the Canada Council
for the Arts, and the Province of British Columbia through the
British Columbia Arts Council and the Book Publishing Tax Credit.

26 25 24 23 22   1 2 3 4 5

Printed in Canada

To my family, with love. Only you know how many times I made nettle pesto pizza on thick whole wheat crust, served in sloppy wedges to eat at Sandwell Beach.

Thank you for all the feasts.

"All sorrows are less with bread."

MIGUEL DE CERVANTES SAAVEDRA

"When you cook for people,
they feel cared for."

RUTH REICHL

*My Kitchen Year: 136 Recipes
That Saved My Life*

CONTENTS

AUTHOR'S NOTE

SEVERAL PEOPLE'S NAMES have been changed, some at their request. Some family members have different recollections of our past, although I have tried my best to recount my life story to the best of my own memories. I had to compress some timelines for clarity of the storyline. Any mistakes I have made are my own, as much of this story was written many years (up to thirty!) after some events occurred.

INTRODUCTION

THE NIGHT I ran over Rick with my car, I was over four months pregnant with our first daughter. I remember crouching at his side, knees painfully ground into the concrete, as I swayed over him in my grief. I didn't know it then—that is was too late. An invisible cord was tethering us, not just me to the baby, but all of us wound up together, pulsing toward everything that came after.

Earlier that night, I had made a vegetarian lasagna. Rick was two hours late. I couldn't call him from our rental suite because we had cancelled our phone service in advance of a move to our new condo, closer to downtown Victoria, near the Galloping Goose Trail.

I walked downstairs to call Rick from the suite below. It was occupied by an unhappy single mom. I often heard her yelling at her timid preschooler through the thin floors covered in shag carpeting running the length of the '70s style rancher. She was a heavy woman, and I imagined her jowls shaking with the effort. I made no attempt to hide my emotions, bonded as we were under the same roof of sorrow.

She let me into her suite, unperturbed by my distressed state. Mothers, I surmised by her bemused expression, must ready themselves for disaster. I hardly registered much of the surroundings as I dialed Rick's cell phone number, hands shaking, fingers still pungent with garlic. He was out for a drink at Sidney's Blue Peter Pub with his crew after the dive. That night he had been seeking small green urchins found on the murky bottom of the ocean, surprisingly close to home for once. I told him not to bother coming home. He took this to mean he didn't have to come back *immediately*.

Yet why *didn't* he know? Most nights I couldn't sleep for the baby kicking me in the bladder. I was sure my fat cells were multiplying each night as I lay sweating on the mattress. I could only take short shallow breaths while the baby dug into my diaphragm and Rick snored, oblivious to my discomfort.

I felt even more alone with that untouched, perfect lasagna. I flashed forward to my baby's birth and everything that would come after. *Who would be there for me then?* My own mother had died when I was twenty-three years old, skeletal from cancer. She wasn't there to warn me against marrying someone whose job takes them up and down the west coast for half of each year. Would I have listened if she had protested? Who listens to their mother when it comes to love?

RICK IS a west coast urchin diver. The ocean is his element, where he is most at home. He is away for weeks at a time harvesting spiny sea urchins that in turn would feed our family. The painful urchin spines get lodged under the skin of his fingers and sometimes his pale freckled legs. He picks at them with a sewing needle he sterilizes with a red plastic lighter. I swear when I step on them, shocked to find them carelessly lodged in the loops of the carpet.

Some dives he catches a Puget Sound king crab and brings it home. The crab scrabbles at the sides of a taped-up Styrofoam cooler. It is Rick's job to kill it with a swift knock to its thick shell, then to deftly slice it in half with a sharp knife. He turns its sweet flesh into mounds of crab cakes, which we feast on, hot and greasy from the pan. Afterward, we sit contentedly on the deck, my bare feet in his lap until the stars come out.

Rick has been a diver since he was nineteen. He has dived for geoducks (giant clams) blasted out of the ocean floor with a strong jet of water. He has collected scallops, sea cucumbers, giant Pacific octopus, and green and red sea urchins. Urchins are hand-picked from rocky crevices with a metal rake, custom fitted to his arm. He holds a large net bag in the other hand while he swims along the seabed up to eight hours a day.

"I make all my money by putting the red ball in the basket," he likes to joke. His right forearm is huge, like the claw of a crab, from filling a 250-pound bag. It's the same arm that will rock our infant daughter to sleep at night with such tenderness.

When I saw Rick finally drive up in his blue truck, I rushed to my car and cursed as I drove straight into his side door just as he was stepping out. I was blind with rage, perhaps more at my alcoholic father than at Rick. He fell to the pavement, orange hair splayed in the swaying shadows of the shifting tree branches. I ran to him, terrified that I had just killed the father of my unborn child.

When I called out to him, voice cracking, he opened his eyes, and said, "I'm okay. It's alright. I'm okay."

I swore at him with a fresh surge of anger. I hauled my body back into the car and sped off wildly, gravel spitting beneath the tires. Small rocks hit his bare legs as he stood dazed, watching me drive away into the night.

I drove to a nearby 7-Eleven and bought a pack of cigarettes, even though I had quit when I first found out I was pregnant. I rented a hotel room off Dallas Road with an ocean view, although I never opened the curtains. I smoked a couple of cigarettes zealously, then fell exhausted on the polyester bed cover, feeling sick and hungry. I wished I'd brought that lasagna.

I FEEL Rick's absence most keenly at night, imagining his powerful body moving in slow motion, silently like a crab, across the cold moonscape of the ocean floor. Even though I am not the one underwater, I feel like I am holding my breath, waiting for disaster. On nights like these, I hope my love will keep him safe. On the many, many nights like these, when I lie alone listening to the hum and chug of the refrigerator—the only sound in our island home—doubt creeps in. I wonder if the amount of pain in our relationship is equal to the amount of joy. Yet Ernest Hemingway said in *A Moveable Feast,* "If you are lucky enough to have lived in Paris as a young man, then wherever you go for the rest of your life, it stays with you, for Paris is a moveable feast." And what feasts we've had.

KILLER LASAGNA
(GARLICKY VEGETARIAN LASAGNA)

This recipe takes a bit of time, but it is worth the trouble. This veggie lasagna is brimming with vitamins and minerals from the big mix of vegetables and will give you plenty of leftovers. A whole roasted garlic bulb makes this recipe over-the-top garlicky and delicious.

Making this meal is an act of love. I guarantee if there is a bubbling, homemade, cheesy lasagna in the oven when your husband walks in from a long day of work, or your daughter returns from running practice, or _____ (fill in the blank), eyes will light up with gratitude.

Makes 1 lasagna, enough to feed 6 people, with leftovers

1 whole garlic bulb
Olive oil
1 large eggplant

Salt
1 package (375-g) dried lasagna noodles

Filling

1½ cups chopped spinach and baby arugula lettuce mix (or any greens you have handy, such as kale or Swiss chard)
¼ cup chopped parsley

1 egg
1 (500-g) container delicate, traditional ricotta cheese
1½ cups mozzarella cheese
½ cup Parmesan cheese, grated is best

Marinara sauce

3 Tbsp olive oil, divided
½ lb mushrooms, sliced
1 large white onion, chopped
1 tsp salt, plus more to taste
1 small green pepper, chopped
1 zucchini, diced
2 large garlic cloves, minced
1 tsp pepper, plus more to taste
1 tsp or so red chili flakes, plus more for sprinkling

2 tsp dried basil
2 tsp dried or fresh oregano
¼ tsp ground thyme (or a sprig of fresh thyme leaves)
2 (796 mL/28 oz each) cans canned plum tomato puree, crushed or diced
2 tsp balsamic vinegar

Finishing the lasagna

1½ cups grated mozzarella cheese, divided

1 cup grated Parmesan cheese, divided

Preheat oven to 425°F. Cut a small amount off the top of the bulb of unpeeled garlic. Lightly toss garlic in a drizzle of olive oil and wrap in foil. Place bulb of garlic in the oven. Roast whole garlic while you are prepping and baking the eggplant. When the garlic is finished roasting (about forty minutes), let cool and then squeeze the softened cloves out of the skin and set aside.

While garlic is roasting slice the eggplant lengthwise into thin 1½ cm pieces Leave skin on and salt generously. Let the salted eggplant rest for 7 minutes to draw out the moisture, and then pat dry with a paper towel. Flip and salt eggplant pieces again. Wait another 7 minutes or so and pat dry once more. Once oven is preheated, add eggplant slices to a greased sheet pan and cook for 10–12 minutes on each side or until lightly browned. Remove pan from oven and set aside until it is time to layer. Turn oven temperature down to 375°F.

Cook lasagna noodles in boiling water (add 1 Tbsp salt) until al dente (10 minutes or so). Drain and rinse pasta with cold water and toss with a bit of oil to prevent the noodles from sticking together.

For the filling
Chop up the spinach, arugula, and parsley. In a bowl, beat the egg and mix into the ricotta cheese ½ cup of the Parmesan cheese. Stir the chopped greens and the 1½ cups grated mozzarella into the ricotta mixture and refrigerate until you are ready to assemble.

For the marinara sauce
Heat 2 Tbsp of olive oil in a large pot and fry up the mushrooms for a few minutes, then add the onions and 1 tsp of

salt and fry until soft. Next, add the chopped green pepper, zucchini, and minced garlic. Stir in the spices (pepper, chili flakes, basil, oregano, thyme) and canned tomatoes, plus balsamic vinegar and 1 more Tbsp of olive oil. Bring to a boil, then reduce to a simmer over medium-high heat for about 35 minutes or until the sauce has thickened. Stir with a wooden spoon. Never use a metal spoon in a tomato-based sauce. Season the sauce with more salt and pepper, if needed. Some people may find the Parmesan cheese adds enough salt, but a bit of extra saltiness brings out the robust flavours. For those who like a spicier sauce, add more black pepper, or sprinkle each portion with extra red chili flakes.

If you haven't already, grate your mozzarella and the additional Parmesan cheese and set aside until you are ready to assemble your lasagna.

Find a large 13 × 9–inch casserole dish or, if you don't have one, use a roasting pan which will allow plenty of room for all your layers, so the contents won't overflow onto the bottom of the oven.

How to layer in order:

1. Cover the bottom of the pan with about ½ cup marinara sauce.

2. Add a layer of cooked lasagna noodles.

3. Spread half of the ricotta cheese/mozzarella and greens mixture.

4. Add the pieces of whole roasted garlic and spread evenly on top of the ricotta mixture. (Rough chunks of caramelized garlic dotted throughout the lasagna are a wonderful surprise to bite into.)

5. Spread another layer of marinara sauce.

6. Layer with slices of roasted eggplant, then sprinkle with ½ cup Parmesan cheese and (chili flakes optional).

7. Add another layer of lasagna noodles.

8. Layer with the rest of the ricotta/mozzarella cheese and greens mixture.

9. Spread more marinara (about 1½ cups).

10. Add the final layer of lasagna noodles.

11. Use up the rest of the marinara sauce.

12. Top with the rest of the mozzarella cheese and remaining ½ cup of grated Parmesan.

Bake for 20 minutes. Rotate the pan and bake for another 20 minutes. Remove from the oven and let set for at least 10 minutes. Dig in.

BOOK BURNING AND
OTHER CAMPFIRE STORIES

MY FIRST MEMORY from childhood is lying in bed, listening through the walls to the murmuring voice of my mother, Ella, talking on the phone to her best friend, Sonia, punctuated by the sound of pages being ripped from my father's paperback books. I was three and too young to understand that she was destroying his books because they were valuable to him. I imagined the long cord following her around as she went back for more volumes. I fell asleep to the sound of her voice rising and falling.

We lived on the top floor of a three-storey walk up. I was woken up by her hands yanking me out of bed. She set me outside the apartment in the building's hallway. The pile of books in the middle of the living room floor reminded me of the leaves I had jumped in that fall. They were on fire. She had called the fire department when my father had come home drunk and set the pile aflame. That is what Sonia told me.

I don't recall being worried; I trusted my mother completely and knew no harm would come to me if she was around. I stood in my white panties and matching undershirt that summer night and was thrilled when a squadron of firemen in their uniforms filed past me on their way to our apartment. They smiled and said hello as they walked by. I felt very special. I didn't realize they may have pitied me—a toddler standing barefoot in the hallway while her parents' fiery marriage imploded in a pile of ashes.

That night I was sent to my father's mother, whom we called Little Baba to differentiate her from my other grandmother, Big Baba. Little Baba's maiden name was as long as she was short—Antoinette Zapotoczny. After she married, she became plain old Anne Fedoruk. She lived down the street with my grandfather in a clean but bare one-storey house on Burrows Avenue in the north end of Winnipeg. She tucked me into bed under flannel sheets smelling of Baby's Own soap and said "Goodnight *kitsenu*," which she told me meant kitten in Ukrainian.

I enjoyed spending time with Little Baba. For lunch she served me Klik (canned lunch meat) sandwiches on doughy slices of Wonder Bread, with the crusts cut off. For a treat, she would walk us to the corner of Burrows and Sinclair to Striker's Deli and Meats. It was a decrepit-looking building, even more dismal in the shadow of the ornate domed church of the Ukrainian Orthodox Cathedral. Before Little Baba left the house, she would tie a white polyester kerchief, a modern-style babushka, under her chin to hold in her curls, the result of a monthly standing hair appointment. I clung to her bony fingers in fear when we entered the dark, windowless cavern that smelled of garlic and other spices. She would carefully select a coil of Polish sausage, called kielbasa, which my grandfather liked to pronounce with a funny voice, "*Koo*-ba-saw."

Later, we ate it sliced with thin-skinned *holubtsi* (cabbage rolls) that she purchased from some industrious Ukrainian ladies who sold them by the dozen from the kitchen in the basement of the church. Cooking was not part of Little Baba's repertoire; she preferred restaurants, hands down. Although in her tiny kitchen, she served me food with love and care. All the cutlery in her kitchen drawers were mysteriously individually hand-wrapped in white paper napkins, like the dried Matzah crackers that we hunted for Passover feasts across town at my other grandparents. Their two worlds were miles apart in food and practices, although I relished whatever meal was placed in front of me. As I grew older, I detected an undercurrent of animosity between the two families, but I never suspected where it stemmed from. I didn't learn about the conflict until much later.

In the years that followed Little Baba would be the one cheering me on in plays. (I was always in the chorus because of my quiet voice.) Or if I was fighting with my mother, which was often, Little Baba would tell me to call a cab and come over, her treat. When I grew older, she pestered me to meet her for lunch at least once a week. She craved hot dogs from Kelekis Restaurant or begged me to meet her at Grapes on Main after I had introduced her to fettucine alfredo, which she couldn't get enough of. Her food had to be the right consistency, in other words, soft enough for her to eat with the few teeth she had left to chew with. She covered her mouth when she laughed to hide her missing and rotten teeth. I don't know why she didn't get them fixed; she may have been afraid of dentists. She encouraged me to get my teeth checked often and insisted on paying my dental bills. Little Baba was always there when I needed her, not just for free lunches and dentist appointments. I relied on her kindness when I was at war with my mother. I considered her one of my best friends.

I HAVE a small snippet of my mother captured on a silent film. She is smoking on a lounge chair as I run around naked on the grassy lawn. I am shocked to see her smoking, my tidy and careful mother. She rarely drank, and only socially in small doses, but every man she chose was a drunk.

I admired her slenderness and beauty, I longed to look like her. My mother's nose was a tiny ski lift with a gentle curve—perfect. It was oh so dainty, while my nose has a detestable hump. My mother had Olivia Newton-John's nose in *Grease,* and I had Barbra Streisand's nose in *The Way We Were.* (In my mind, Streisand's character lost handsome Robert Redford because of her gargantuan nose.) I spent years hating my nose, applying makeup to the bump to make it fade away. In photographs of me in preadolescence, I have so much white makeup on, my face blurs into the white background. I was trying to erase myself. I was chubby and had what my mother referred to as "baby fat." I felt lumpy and ungainly in my polyester pants, cinched up too high to prevent their bell-bottoms from dragging in the dirt. When I was ten years old, I took grapefruit pills to counter my pudginess. Meanwhile, my mother had put me in ballet lessons to instill some grace. I developed some lasting dance moves but never lost the weight. My mother didn't need to exercise; she was always trim, and her nose, oh, her nose. More than anything, I longed for a nose like hers.

At night I held down the bump on my nose with thumb and forefinger, my version of Chinese foot binding, hoping the bump would cease to grow, would be forced into submission. When I grew weary, my sore nose and I fell into a fitful sleep. I longed to look like my mother, yet little did I know then that her nose was the result of rhinoplasty when she was seventeen years old.

By the time I learned about her nose job, my only source of information was my mother's childhood friend, Sonia. Sonia's father worked in the back room of my zayda's (grandfather's) furrier shop.

"Listen, Margot, it was all the rage back then," Sonia said.

She began all of her stories, with "Listen," to command an audience, and then she always gave me a warning,

"Are you sure you want to hear the truth about your mother?" she said.

I admired her ability to draw out the drama, making me sit on the edge of my seat and beg for the story. She was an expert.

"Yes! Please tell me what you know," I said.

Her voice made my own throat constrict, reminding me of my mother, how she would slip into a mock Yiddish accent when she was on the phone with her Jewish friends, a handful of women she had known her whole life.

"Believe it or not, Manitoba Health paid for a nose job. Everyone was doing it. You just had to sign a form explaining you had trouble breathing. Even I got one," Sonia told me.

The more I listened, the more convinced I became that my mother's drive to change her looks ran deeper than wanting to fix her large foreign-looking nose. My mother was born in Russia in a small town in 1943. Her father was Meyer Zahn, a Polish Jew who met my grandmother, Neura, while he was chopping firewood. Their story was like the beginning of one of the fables I read under my down comforter at night as a child.

Neura (whom we called Big Baba) was a blonde-haired, blue-eyed Slavic beauty in desperate need of a good reliable man. She had been left by her mother to be raised by her grandmother. She had only minimal education. Neura was drawn to Meyer because he was not anything like her last two men—boisterous, hard-drinking husbands whom she had lost during the Second World War, leaving her with a small son to raise. Meyer was just what the doctor ordered, gentle and quiet, and he had a trade. When I study pictures of the before in my mother's before-and-after life, I can see she had Meyer's nose, large protruding ears, and dark hair.

As a child, I loved visiting my zayda's furrier shop, Boston Fur Company, on Main Street in Winnipeg. I was allowed to visit the dark back room where the men sat at their sewing machines next to the strong sweet-smelling fur, their aroma wafting up from the piles of pelts. When I was younger, I had received white fur earmuffs for Christmas and a handmade stuffed dog.

Growing up in a Jewish neighbourhood in Winnipeg with my friend Rhonda Gillman meant we'd spend our time roller skating to the synagogue at the end of our street, navigating the small incline as our cheap skates stretched over our shoes uncomfortably. If it was raining, we lounged on her carpeted living room floor playing Clue (we both wanted to be stylish Miss Scarlet). When we grew tired of board games, we made up our own songs, lyrics included.

I will never forget this little ditty:

Yesterday I met a cutie and he said how do you doodie.
Nah nah nah.
I said fine and turned around and then he saw my nose and frowned.
Nah nah nah.
My big schnoz.
Nah nah nah.
Please break it!

We belted it out, rolling on the floor, holding our cheeks in pain. Jewish girls were trained to hate their large noses. My mother had told me when I turned sixteen, I could get a nose job. I'll admit that I was tempted, but as I grew older, I couldn't imagine having an operation to fix something that wasn't broken. My mother also had her floppy ears "pinned back." For as long as I can remember, she dyed her "cow-shit brown" hair blonde.

Then Sonia told me another story of compromise that was much worse. My mother was waiting for an engagement ring on Valentine's Day—she was only seventeen. When it didn't come, she had a fit.

Later that summer, she and Sonia were sitting on the front steps of my mother's family townhouse on Atlantic Avenue in Winnipeg when the phone rang. It was Mrs. Fedoruk, my father's mother. She said, "It's nothing personal, but you can't be with my son. He can't marry a Jewish girl. He's Catholic. He was an altar boy. You leave him alone."

My mother ran to the bathroom and threw up.

"That was the start of her stomach ailments," Sonia said. "I believe that's what killed her in the end—stress. But your mother didn't give up. She was a beautiful force to be reckoned with."

Sonia believes my father never loved my mother. "It was a marriage made in hell," Sonia said candidly. She talks in cliches. "You got the short end of the stick. Your sister got the shorter end of the stick. Your mother loved your father, but he never really loved her back. It was like beating a dead horse. She couldn't force him to love her."

My mother's nose job was an effort to be less Jewish and more Catholic. If Frank's mother—born and raised in Winnipeg, a churchgoer without an accent—wanted her to fit in, she would do it, even if she had to keep it up for the rest of her days. She overhauled her appearance and, so help her God, she muscled her way into my father's Catholic altar-boy arms. It was a *Romeo and Juliet* love story, especially since my mother's parents also did not want them to marry.

Was I more like my mother than I thought when I fell in love with Rick? No one wants to be like their mother. I'll never know why I chose to raise a family with a deep-sea diver, but I did, and I pay the price again and again. I worry that Rick won't come back from a fishing trip, will be eaten by a killer whale, or be attacked by aggressive sea lions. I worry that a hungover dive tender will cut his air tank lines. Around the campfire, people beg to hear his near-miss stories, but I feel as sick to my stomach as my mother did when her almost-fiancé's mother called, and she went nose to nose with destiny.

Sonia told me another story to help me understand my parent's tumultuous past. She said my mother sat at the kitchen table in the duplex on Atlantic Avenue with her parents, against the backdrop of floor-to-ceiling windows that lit up the whole kitchen, lace curtains breathing in and out with the breeze. I pictured Big Baba washing dishes, wiping down the counters, stirring pots, feeding people. The purpose of this meeting was to convince my mother not to marry my father because of the violence.

I was shocked. "What kind of violence?" I asked Sonia.

"Your Little Baba really got it bad from your grandfather when he was drinking," she said. There were weekends he went on benders, borrowing money from the business to gamble and carouse. How had I not known that when he came home drunk, he hit her?

My mother's parents worried that serious problems, including the drinking and gambling, would repeat itself.

My mother at seventeen years old, smoking on the sly to keep her figure, wouldn't have believed it possible then, but after ten years of marriage to Frank (Francis) Fedoruk, and on her deathbed, she did. My father had been unfaithful to my mother, gambled, and drank himself out of a high-paying government job in the Winnipeg legislature building. Yet he had a gentle side. He was also a black-haired scholar, his large Ukrainian nose always stuffed in a paperback, while he sat legs crossed, chain smoking, ignoring the world around him. He was kind, loved the underdog, and was generous to a fault. He listened to rap music in the '80s, said I should listen to the lyrics because they were singing about an important social movement. But his kindness couldn't override his addictions, couldn't stop him from acting out the same mistakes of his own father, just as Big Baba and Zayda had predicted.

WHILE WE played Parcheesi in Rhonda Gillman's living room, I watched enviously as she fought with her sister or brothers. I had the same feeling sitting on the front steps of a rented vacation cabin in Ontario, watching longingly as the kids across the way played tag barefoot in the grass. There was no comparison, just as our accommodations paled in contrast: our two-room affair with a musty cot in a cramped kitchenette, complete with hot plate and sink littered with dead spiders compared to their palatial two-storey cabin.

In an effort to extend my family and staunch my loneliness, I named everything, from my dusty ceramic ornaments to the stars in the dark cold prairie nights when it felt like they were my only friends winking down at me. I named the trees in our front yard on McAdam Avenue (Giovanni and Gwendolyn) inspired by the characters in books I read under my blankets with a flashlight most nights. I was mad for fairy tales, the original ones, with maidens who washed their hands in milk and were valued for their kindness. I couldn't get enough of the story about the sisters who snuck out to dance all night and wrecked their shoes. I also overate and watched endless sitcoms while my mother argued with my father about his "gallivanting around," meaning sex with other women.

One night while listening to their yelling match in the bedroom next to mine, I brazenly barged in and lied, "I had a bad dream! I was stuck on the top of a Ferris wheel, and I couldn't get down."

This was the plot of a movie I had watched alone the night before. I pinched myself to make tears. It worked. They quit fighting, and I was tucked under the down comforter in my single bed so tightly it was if my mother meant to pin me there with fabric.

When my mother got pregnant, I wondered if that was what they had been fighting about. Now I wouldn't be lonesome in a house simmering with resentments; I would have company, a partner in the struggle. I was ecstatic. I didn't know my mother had lost a baby a few years earlier.

I remember sitting cross-legged in a circle across from my classmate, an angelic-faced boy with sky blue eyes, when Mrs. Smith, my Grade 1 teacher, received a phone call and told the whole class, "Margot has a new little sister!"

I was wearing a yellow happy face T-shirt and bursting with happiness inside and out. When Tanya came home in a white flannel blanket, her tiny head wobbled on her neck.

She was pale with a dark fringe of hair, as opposed to my fair hair that lightened each summer to blonde. My mother set Tanya's sleepy head on my warm lap, and I patted her bony back, watching episodes of *Black Beauty* in the basement. My heart hurt with the tenderness of her shuddering breaths, bubbles of spit on her pink lips. I gently touched her tiny earlobes with the tip of my finger, unable to believe I had my own living doll.

I took my job seriously as a big sister. If Donna, the babysitter, ignored Tanya's cries, I would sit next to her crib and rub tiny circles on her back, switching arms if one grew sore.

Donna came from two doors over, and had unkempt black hair and a big appetite, opening and closing the kitchen cupboards while she hunted for cookies. She went to the basement with her loot to watch TV while I took over.

Tanya grew and began to follow me everywhere. I had someone to join me on Halloween, traipsing through the neighbourhood, so I made her costume by hand, using my mother's Singer sewing machine. I was Dorothy and she was Toto.

I fretted when her elbow, prone to slipping out of its joint, caused her to wince in pain. It only took a snap to get it back into place, but until we learned that, we relied on heating pads and comforting her with thick chocolate pudding, stirred up on the stovetop. Big Baba's Russian friends recommended a traditional folk remedy for Tanya's itchy, raw skin on her feet. She complained when we wrapped a plastic bag of sliced onions on her cracked feet at night. The bags were stolen from the vegetable section of Dominion Foods.

I was there for her when she first sleepwalked. My mother and I nervously trailed her around the house as she made noises like a chimpanzee, with a fuzzy far-away look in her eyes. My mother heard it was dangerous to wake a person sleepwalking, and imagined she would go into shock or fall into a coma.

I too had a habit of trying to escape in this state in the dead of winter in my flannel nightgown and bare feet. Maybe I was subconsciously looking for a new, better family. Once I squatted in the corner of the bathroom to relieve myself. When my mother woke me up to get me to pee on the toilet, I came back to the real world and saw her standing under the glaring lights, her thin frame shivering in her silky nightgown. She sought medical advice from other mothers or from her mother's friends from the old country about our sleepwalking. She would try anything to get us to stay put.

Tanya was the sister I had been longing for, for seven long, lonely years. I used to think up exciting games for us to play, nicking a pillowcase from my mother's laundry basket and going "tiger hunting" for our cat. When I was at school all day, I would come home to find Tanya had gotten into my Barbie dollhouse, the one I spent hours making out of a series of cardboard boxes and playing cards and bits and pieces of material for curtains. I had colourful toothpick umbrellas for my dolls to lounge under, nicked from fancy cocktails, but Tanya turned them inside out, breaking their tiny frames. She would chew on my Barbie's feet until she reached bone. When I returned home from school and discovered all the destruction, like Godzilla had razed through a corner of my flowery bedroom, I would yell, "Mom! You said you would keep Tanya out of my bedroom!" I wished I had a lock on my door.

I hardly stayed mad for long though. At night we would listen to the radio station on the stereo from my mom's new boyfriend, Clancy. We listened to "Funky Town" and danced around the living room. I would hold Tanya's small, sweaty hands and bounce her on my mother's pristine couch to the beat of the music, and then tuck her into bed.

My parents' faltering marriage had failed, and in between their divorce and my mother finding romance with other men, first Clancy and then Ronald, she joined Parents Without Partners. Eventually, she brought home a handsome Black boyfriend who gave her emerald earrings for Christmas and a Fleetwood Mac album for me. I have an entry in my diary, "Guess what, mom's new boyfriend is married. Isn't that hilarious?" When she found this out, my mother called his wife to let her know what was going on. I remember listening to the call from my perch on the carpeted stairs. This confrontation made my stomach twist, but I couldn't tear myself away from the drama. Later, I wanted to run from her drama.

As my mother's behaviour got louder and stronger, I became quieter. I whispered and was constantly asked to speak up. I could never stand up to her. I gave in easily because I knew she would always win. Sometimes I came home to find her ripping my posters off the wall, telling me she was sick and tired of my filthy room.

SITTING AT my mother's bedside twenty years later, I noticed her pale skin and the dark circles under her eyes. She hid the cancer so she could apply for life insurance. She hadn't said the C-word, but I knew she was very ill. Still, I couldn't help complaining about her current husband, Ronald.

"How could you love *him*?" I asked.

"I loved your father and look where that got me," she said in tears. *Why love if you can be broken by it?* These words haunted me for decades.

She would die soon afterward, on a cold day in February. I don't remember much after that. I know that before her memorial, Tanya and I played Scrabble at the kitchen table to keep our minds off the eerie absence of our mother. Ronald was madly cleaning the already spotless house and demanded that we help. He had purchased two tickets to Hawaii to help motivate my mother to get better. But her cancer had other plans. Ronald asked if one of us wanted to use the non-refundable ticket. He couldn't find anyone to go with him— no one from his family, not even his own sons. We declined.

When he and my mother got married in Hawaii, he had got so lit he mistook their suitcase for a toilet to relieve himself. I couldn't imagine joining someone who drank so much they couldn't locate the bathroom, even for a free trip. When Ronald called me into the living room to yell about some small infraction, I coped by watching him from a murky distance. I had learned to let my mind wander as Ronald furiously spouted angry words until his face turned borscht red. I knew I had to get Tanya out of there.

I also knew I would not follow in my parents' footsteps. I would not drag my children into any family drama. There would be no misery. There would be only love and understanding. I would not make their same mistakes.

MY ZAYDA, Meyer Zahn, had a wallet overflowing with money every fall when the cool weather crept back onto the Prairies. That's when he collected payment for keeping his clients' fur coats in cold storage. Meyer picked up the fur coats in the spring to deliver them to a plant to be stored at a special temperature. In the fall, he would return them, and his clients would pay him in cash.

"Zayda was usually a poor man," my uncle Harvey told me. "It was only in September that he couldn't close his wallet."

I can almost smell the leather wallet, the same animal smell that wafted from the back of his shop, the Boston Fur Company. It was the same brown wallet he would pull out during Passover meals to reward his grandkids for finding the matzahs, large tasteless crackers that Big Baba broke apart in different size pieces and wrapped in white cloth napkins, which she hid around the house. When we found the matzah, we presented them to Zayda at his customary spot at the head of the dining table. We stood in line in anticipation of him giving us a ten, twenty, or fifty dollar bill in exchange for the matzah. I got the most money because I was the eldest. I looked forward to this tradition as much as I enjoyed hunting for chocolate eggs hidden beneath the couch cushions during Easter celebrations at home. Big Baba tried her best to recreate traditional Jewish fare, but her matzah balls were heavy as golf balls. The star of the meal was always her homemade perogies which she hauled steaming out of the kitchen by the dozen. We ate until we groaned in blissful agony.

Meyer had first worked at a fur factory in Winnipeg called Stall's. He was famous in his family for saying, "I don't do left sleeves," meaning he was not an assembly line worker. He left soon after to start a business with Moynick Reisman. Everyone wore furs in Winnipeg for protection from the frigid winters—just like the winters back home in Russia, Ukraine, Czechoslovakia, Germany, and Poland. I loved visiting Zayda's shop on Main Street.

My other grandfather, William Fedoruk, had a store two doors away called Ideal Produce, a corner store with shelves lined with dusty canned soup. The store included an egg delivery business, with a grading facility in the back. Bill, as Little Baba called him, owned the whole building, which is why I was treated like a princess each time I visited. Everyone stopped what they were doing to say hello. I would stand in the shop window next to a mannequin and hold still, clearly not fooling anyone. I was allowed to remove staples with a special tool in the back of Ideal Produce, and the ladies who worked there showed me how to grade eggs with a little green light.

William Fedoruk was taciturn. I don't recall ever spending any time with him. He was the quiet type, typical of ex-alcoholics who were not drinking anymore. He drove Little Baba and me around in his Cadillac with a bump that looked like the back end of a turkey. We drove to Eaton's or the Hudson's Bay Company to shop for his boxers.

"Why can't he buy his own underwear?" I asked Little Baba.

He sat in the car listening to the radio while we scoped out Barbie doll outfits for my large collection. Little Baba's house had plain white walls, no pictures. Plain like how she dressed; she favoured black polyester pants, which she referred to as slacks. She was tiny, with a hawkish nose, brilliant blue eyes. She told me that when she was a teenager, they called her Tiny Tina.

In contrast, Big Baba and Zayda lived in a duplex in West Kildonan, a suburb of Winnipeg, where we were allowed to crawl around on the furniture, try on sequined gowns, wrap our necks in real fur, and paint our toenails red. They always had ice cream cones—richness in my mind. My mother would never waste money on cones for ice cream when you could eat from a bowl. Big Baba had orange tongue-staining pop from Pic-a-Pop. The soft drinks came in plastic crates filled with glass bottles you could return to refill. They had wall-to-wall carpets, and each room was wallpapered in vibrant reds and golds with raised velvet curlicues, and a fleur-de-lis motif. There was never a hint of dust anywhere. After washing the dishes, I was instructed to hang the dishcloth outside on the line or it would "get schtinky." There was nothing old in their home on Hartford Avenue, no secondhand furniture, no used clothing.

My zayda would sometimes drive with us stuffed in the back of his station wagon, the back window rolled down a crack so we could breathe. We sat wedged between the beach blankets, an enormous oblong watermelon, and a covered basket of breaded chicken wings and thick potato latkes (pancakes) that we would eat cold on our picnic at Winnipeg Beach on a sweltering hot day. After we ate, we were instructed to wait a painstakingly long half-hour before we were allowed to swim in the tiny waves of Lake Winnipeg.

Meyer Zahn was my favourite grandfather. He never raised his voice; he was patient and kind.

In the evenings, he would sit quietly as my baba served him red sickly sweet crab apple compote. When I turned up my nose, she would admonish me, "Ay, you are bad girl. Compote is good. Your zayda loves it."

He dutifully ate a bowlful every night before reading the newspaper while she bustled about the kitchen. She took on the job of feeding the family with a vengeance. It was difficult to fend off her advances; most of the time I ate to bursting just to keep her off my back. If she served Jell-O for dessert, she would reply to my moaning with "Here, eat it. It's nothing, like air."

"Why Baba? If I'm not hungry, why do I have to eat?"

She would put it in on the table in front of me, forcing me to eat a spoonful even when I wanted to vomit. Her father died of starvation during the Russian Revolution. He was found on a train, ribs protruding, like the pictures of Jews in the concentration camps. Her mission was to make sure everyone was well fed; she would not lose anyone on her watch.

Recently, when I video called my uncle Harvey, their youngest son, to ask him some questions, I was reminded of my zayda, with his big Jewish nose, and tall willowy body. Unlike my zayda, Harvey has a booming voice. He told me Meyer left his home in Poland during the Second World War when they were forced to wear black armbands to signal that they were Jews. He wanted to escape the oppression and hopefully find work somewhere in Russia. He left with his brother for the train station. My sister thinks they had to crawl through the sewers to get to there, but these family stories are often embellished for dramatic effect. In the confusing throng of people at the station, Zayda lost his brother. Zayda continued on to Russia and never saw his brother again.

At the end of the war, Meyer returned to Poland and could find not a single member of his forty-person extended family. He stopped believing in God shortly afterward.

Despite all of his hardships and losses, he never appeared bitter or angry. He taught me songs. I would repeat after him in Polish: "Here is the church and here is the steeple, open the doors and see all the people," as our fingers wiggled like people.

My ability to speak or understand Polish has faded like his memory. He started hallucinating and accused Big Baba of infidelity. One day, I was locked out of the house and had to use the neighbour's phone to ask him to pick me up, but he misunderstood and drove to the downtown library. Oh, the pain and embarrassment. I was ashamed about the confusion, and soon afterward he slipped into Parkinson's. To me, it was as if he just stayed angry about our miscommunication. Years later, when I was training to be a nurse's aide at Camosun College in Victoria, I learned it was the disease that had changed him, but as a young girl I only saw how the early symptoms had twisted his face to anger, and I thought he didn't love me anymore.

Sometimes I wonder if my zayda's disease was a gift—an answer to his request to forget his past. He could forget the day he lost his brother at the train station, the loss of his mother and sisters and the rest of his family in the war. Perhaps Parkinson's was the cold storage of his mind, a place to park the painful parts of his past, when he didn't have the skills or help to deal with them.

ONE WEEKEND when I stayed over, I almost sleepwalked out the front door in my bare feet. It was minus-thirty degrees outside.

"Margot, where are you going?" he said, patiently leading me by the hand back to my warm bed.

The mind is a powerful thing. It guided me down the carpeted steps, put my hand on the cool metal doorknob, had me fumble with the lock.

My mother's friend Sonia's mother was a survivor who also couldn't cope after losing everyone. She couldn't keep the house clean. Sonia never let friends visit, made them wait outside even in a snowstorm. She remembers going to the doctor with her mother as a child and the doctor saying, "You have to choose. Do you want to live your life or not?"

I WANT to be transported to my mother's small kitchen, a small table wedged in the corner, orange flowered wallpaper the backdrop for a scene from *Moonstruck,* in which Cher's character, Loretta, is surrounded by her big Italian family when her mother asks her, "Do you love him, Loretta?" In my version, my mother asks it in a Yiddish accent.

"Ma," I reply, "I love him awful."

BLINTZES

Big Baba called them *blinchikis*, and when Tanya was little, she begged me to roll her up in a blanket and make her into a blintz. In France these thin pancakes are called crepes. Tanya sent me our mother's original recipe typed onto a little recipe card on the same electric typewriter I borrowed to write my essays on Dostoyevsky for my high school English class. My mother also used it to type out a poem about my messiness and left the paper in the roller for me to discover. My mother is talking to me still.

Feel free to substitute half the white flour with organic spelt or light buckwheat flour, if you are feeling hippyish. This will make a heavier blintz, so add extra water to keep the batter nice and thin (only if necessary). It should not be as thick as pancake batter.

Makes 12 blintzes

Butter or oil for frying
3 eggs
1 cup of milk or water (milk is best)
½ tsp salt
2 Tbsp melted butter (plus more for frying)

¾ cup white unbleached flour (see headnote for substitutions for other types of flour)
Fillings: honey, jam, real maple syrup, cottage cheese and strawberry sauce

Heat 2 Tbsp of butter in a 6-inch skillet. In a bowl, beat the eggs, milk, salt, and the melted butter. Stir in the flour with a whisk to get rid of lumps. Pour in approximately 2½ Tbsp of the batter into the heated pan, tilting to coat the bottom. Cook until light brown and flip over to lightly brown the other side. Add extra butter as needed to keep the blintzes from sticking to the pan. Continue making blintzes with the rest of the batter.

Eat hot from the pan rolled up with a slather of honey, jam, or real maple syrup. If you want to get fancy, roll each blintz up with ⅓ cup of drained cottage cheese and pour warm strawberry sauce over top.

TRAVEL TIPS FOR
ANXIOUS CHILDREN

EVERY SUNDAY at 6 PM, the instrumental version of "When You Wish Upon a Star," from *The Magical World of Disney* called me to the castle. Later, head buried under my down comforter, tiny flickers of light formed fireworks beneath my tightly clenched eyelids. When I was ten, I wanted to visit Disneyland more than I wanted a dog.

Every Sunday morning, I spread the pages of the *Winnipeg Free Press* across the living room carpet scanning the Pets for Sale section: Adorable Chow Chow Puppies For Sale. I read this section until my elbows were smudged and itchy with ink.

Later, I would pester my mother for one of those black-tongued puppies while she stood frying hamburger for the spaghetti sauce she would freeze for the week ahead. She stood her ground; my mother wanted a pet-free, immaculate home.

For Christmas in 1976, my father surprised me with a trip to Disney World. My sister was barely three, too young to leave my mother, so it would be a special trip, just the two of us. My parents had been divorced for a few years, and this was my father's grand gesture.

I resented the presence of my mother's new boyfriend, Clancy, in our two-storey bungalow. Clancy had instituted detested new house rules, such as an early bedtime. I missed the way my father would crawl up the carpeted stairs on his hands and knees, snorting like a beast, making me scream in fright as I put my head under the bed covers.

My mother would admonish him, "Frank! Don't rile her up at bedtime!"

I didn't know then that this fun was partly due to his propensity for Crown Royal. I used its purple drawstring bag to store my marble collection or linking plastic monkeys.

Clancy rose only slightly in my esteem when he persuaded Mom to allow us to have an English sheepdog puppy, which was delivered to us on Christmas morning. My mother named her Mandy, after her favourite Barry Manilow song. Mandy ran straight to me, furiously wagging her nubby, cropped tail. I bowed down, unable to resist mashing my face into her fluffy neck, which smelled like crusted snow.

I would whisper the secrets of a lonely, chubby little girl with buck teeth into her fur until Clancy moved out, and Mandy was swiftly dispatched to "some nice people on a farm," where she would have the space to snap at dragonflies as she frolicked over grassy fields.

As it turned out, my father had purchased tickets to Disney World, that lesser-known, Orlando-based evil twin to California's Disneyland—a place where alligators could be lurking in the swamps, snapping from under footbridges at unsuspecting ankles, pudgy and pale from being stuffed into snow pants over long Prairie winters.

On our flight from Winnipeg to Orlando, I impatiently rubbed my irritated nose between thumb and index finger, a habit I had developed in reaction to my father's chainsmoking, even in enclosed elevators, cars, and jets. Yet even that couldn't dampen my excitement about my first holiday away from the ordered world of my mother's prying eyes.

At the gates of Disney World, my father said the sparkling castle was really a haunted house, perhaps a ploy to frighten me out of waiting in another long lineup. The Cinderella Castle, I later learned, was built with something called forced perspective to make it appear taller than it really is; the first level of the castle is built to scale while the second floor is a façade that is five-eighths the size of the first floor.

I was an anxious child—most rides terrified me—so each day I cast nervous glances at the castle, with its drawbridge frozen in place, waiting in line for the Mad Tea Party ride while my father leaned against a fake lamppost chain-smoking Player's Lights.

"Are you having fun?" my father asked.

"I miss my dog," I replied.

I played my first video game, Atari's Pong, in the hotel lobby on a flat screen embedded in a wooden table. My father nipped into the hotel bar while I defended my goal from a ball of light.

Afterward, on the way up in the elevator to our hotel room, I pressed the emergency button in error when someone hollered at me to hold the elevator doors. I bit the inside of my cheek to hold back my tears. I was certain setting off an alarm was a punishable offense.

One day we made our way along the South Orange Blossom Trail to Gatorland. When we got there, my father had them take two photographs of us and paid extra for the cheap cardboard frames. One photo is of my father, holding a small, muzzled alligator; the other is of me with a clammy-skinned snake around my neck, my face pasty white. No death-defying rides on this trip, just hungry alligators and snakes that might swallow you whole.

I stood next to throngs of tourists, thrilled and nervous from my perch on a bridge, camera poised to take blurry photos as the park attendants dangled dead chickens on what looked like fishing lines to feed the alligators. Their mouths were surprisingly tender-pink when their jaws swiped at the slippery meat.

On New Year's Eve, Dad left me at a ramshackle house belonging to the father of a woman he had just met. I sat on a loveseat next to her scrawny young daughter who regaled me with shockingly erotic tales, while her grandfather watched TV. Cockroaches skittered between the Christmas cards taped to the wall. I reached down to pet their tiny white poodle but recoiled when I saw its back was alive with fleas.

The grandfather, in a ratty, yellowing undershirt strained over his belly, asked me, "Do ya want anything? Glass of water?"

He lumbered toward me with a glass of tap water, a cockroach clinging to its rim until he nonchalantly flicked it off with the tip of his finger. I took the glass and pretended to take a sip.

"Thank you," I whispered. My eyes teared up with exhaustion as I anxiously waited for my father's return. When we were driving back to the hotel late that night, I recounted the evening's events, which he expertly manufactured into an adventure.

"Cockroaches! Ewwww!" I knew by his mocking tone it was meant to be a secret.

THE NEXT day, Dad told me to remain in the rental car while he visited his new girlfriend.

I sat nervously pondering the sign by the swamp lined with palms: BEWARE OF ALLIGATORS. Dad ran out of the tiny cabin and jumped into the driver's seat, Old Spice cologne following him like a jet's contrail. In his haste to get away, he drove over the curb.

"Her boyfriend's home," he said by way of explanation, as I braced myself with both hands on the dash.

When had my father had time to meet this woman? While I was making myself dizzy on the Mad Tea Party ride? Was this the permed woman working in the wooden stall selling tickets? Did my father leave me alone in our hotel room at night, while I slept fitfully, eyes irritated from his cigarette smoke?

Years later, when I recount this Orlando tale to Rick after a shared bottle of homemade Pinot Noir, I need him to assure me, "No, that was not a very good holiday," just as I know it is my job to assure him that heaven and hell are human constructs and nothing to fear, which is hard for him to separate from his Protestant upbringing.

IN A small, orange-flowered photo album filled with pictures taken with my instant camera, I have a white-bordered photo with the inscription: *Remember New Years in Orlando. Love Dad xo* written in blue ink. I am leaning into my father on a flowered '70s couch. This photo was taken before my parents' divorce; my face is open and trusting as I clutch my Holly Hobbie colouring book.

Was our trip a wild and memorable ride with alligators snapping, and dancing cockroaches—events that would never occur on my mother's watch? Did this mean that men are wild and not to be trusted and women are the keepers of order? Perhaps this is what drew me Rick, his scent like fresh air and salt water, sea kelp and diesel fuel. In those moments I am there at the bottom of the sea with him, in the primal and alien world where he is both hunter and the hunted. I warn my girls, "Never marry a fisherman," but I couldn't help myself.

WHEN I was eight years old, I attended a live auction held at a neighbourhood church, only a short walk down our back lane.

I was mesmerized by the hall full of people seated in folding chairs lined up in rows facing a painting of the Queen. It was standing room only. I had arrived at the church early, and I had a good seat.

It was the same church my elementary school used for PE classes. Every winter day we walked down Smith Street to run thundering laps past that enormous painting of Her Royal Highness. It had been in this hall that Carolyn Flower and I had become best friends. We were locked in the storage room together one day when we were putting away the hula hoops. As we stood in the darkness, rattling the doorknob, it dawned on us that we had been left behind. We laughed so hard tears poured down our cheeks, and we had to squeeze our legs together to avoid wetting our pants.

The night of the auction, I lost all sense of time. I longed for each item up for sale, but I was too terrified to raise my hand. I had one paper dollar to spend, but I couldn't get up the gumption to make a bid. Each teacup and saucer fascinated me, just as the sing-song voice of the auctioneer pulled me into a kind of reverie. How I longed to own a cup with an intricate dragon design or tiny pink vining flowers embossed with gold. Each item was like a treasure in Aladdin's cave.

Suddenly, I realized it was almost ten o'clock, two hours past my bedtime. I scurried out the back lane only to see my mother headed toward me, a fierce look on her face. She would not normally go out in public without dressing gracefully and having her face made up, but here she was wearing a fuzzy old coat that made her look like an alpaca and her hair was sticking up at all angles. And if that was not shocking enough, she was wielding a big stick.

"Where. Have. You. Been?" she said in between swacks. I began to cry, more humiliated than hurt. My mother rarely hit me because I hardly ever dared to do anything to upset her.

MY MOTHER, Ella, worked as a secretary at the local TD Bank down on Main Street and held garage sales all summer long to make extra income. She was fond of classical music and listened to Beethoven's nine symphonies, turning them up so loud that the trumpets made the windows shake. She encouraged me to do well in school and had purchased a set of the Encyclopedia Britannica from the grocery store, two at a time. I kept them lined up neatly on the wooden shelves in my bedroom. Ella had never made it past high school, and I knew she hoped I wouldn't end up a divorcee without prospects. I never lost the feeling that she was displeased with me, and everything I did.

A common refrain was "You're just like your father." She said this in a way that I knew was a criticism. I was never clear on what bad parts I had inherited.

She was always plucking pieces of lint from our house's russet carpets or tidying the junk drawer while she sat at the kitchen table, cradling the phone under her chin. My job was to vacuum the front hallway every day after school to get rid of pesky pine needles, something my mother could not abide.

Ella spent a considerable amount of time and money on professionally framed art prints; one wall had artwork of various sizes reaching up to the ceiling. None of my friends had homes filled with so much art. In the front hallway, on a table at the foot of the stairs, was a bronze statue of *Darwin's Ape* sculpture, perched on a pile of books, eternally studying a human skull. I had no idea what it meant and never thought to ask. My mother had also purchased a large reproduction of de Heem's famous *Vase of Flowers* which she made monthly payments for. I couldn't understand why she had paid so much money for a framed picture hung in the living room, where I wasn't normally allowed.

If she had any extra money, she put it into the rest of the house, wallpapering all of the rooms herself, tying her hair in a cloth turban before industriously steaming off the old wallpaper. The new paper had to be brushed with thick white glue then smoothed with a flat metal ruler to wipe off the excess. The kitchen had washable paper with a dizzying pattern of yellow flowers. Tanya's bedroom walls were crowded with a patchwork of denim squares. I poured over the wallpaper sample book that weighed about a hundred pounds, surveying the mesmerizing choices.

I chose throbbing yellow and orange flowers that rivalled a traditional Ukrainian Easter egg and yellow wall-to-wall carpet to match.

"Are you sure?" she asked again and again, when I had made my wallpaper selection.

I hung a pink-and-yellow Japanese umbrella over my bed. In my teens, I would stumble home late from a party and feel the walls closing in on me, a combination of angry colours and magic mushrooms.

My mother was not an avid reader, unlike my father and I, although she did have a few classics on a shelf over her bed. If I was out of books I would snoop through her small collection and sneak a copy of Judy Blume's, *Wifey*, which was definitely not as good as *Blubber* or *Are You There God? It's Me, Margaret*. I combed through her copy of *Lady Chatterley's Lover*, hoping to find something juicy but was disappointed. I was too young to understand the details.

Mother took me to see *Madame Butterfly* at the Manitoba Theatre Centre, where my dance company held our annual ballet recital. I felt out of place wearing my pink corduroy pants, but I didn't own anything fancier.

Sometimes, my mother couldn't get out of bed because her "back was out," code for "your father is a drunk and a cheat and has left me with two little girls to raise." She kept the blinds closed to keep out the summer sun. We were taught to close the doors quietly without slamming them.

Other mothers served peanut butter-and-jelly sandwiches using white bread, cut into bite-sized triangles. My mother scooped out avocados with the tip of a teaspoon or snacked on a can of oily sardines, silver scales and all. I turned up my nose with disgust.

WHEN I was ten years old and Clancy moved in, he brought with him a love of gourmet food. He and Ella made classic Caesar salad, complete with grainy anchovies, in an enormous wooden bowl rubbed with a clove of raw garlic. In the fridge my mother kept a bowl of gelatinous pickled pig's feet called *kholodets*. Clancy helped dig up the whole corner of the backyard so my mother could plant a vegetable garden. In the fall, she lined the shelves in a corner of the basement with jars of pickles.

For New Year's, my mother would buy live lobsters, claws tied together, their long antennas still wiggling. I would watch in horror as they were boiled alive in a large metal pot. Though the silver nutcracker used to crack open the hard shells fascinated me.

My mother told me a story about the first time she saw the ocean as a small child. Her family had just hiked over the Alps to the safety of Italy with the help of the Jewish Brigade. She ran to the edge of the ocean to scoop up a handful of water to slake her thirst. She was shocked by the salty taste and spit it out. She laughed when she told this story.

I don't recall my mother eating sweets, although as a rare treat she would drive across town to a special Italian bakery to pick up a white cardboard box of cream horns—sweet puff pastries filled with real whipped cream. I would wash them down with large tumblers of milk as I did when I added packets of Carnation Instant Breakfast (as it was then known) to milk most mornings before running down the back lane to school. When I walked into Dominion Foods one day to say hello to my Uncle Harvey, who worked there on the weekends stocking shelves, I was surprised that given my mother's complaints about the quantity of milk we went through each week that it was only seventy-five cents for a bottle.

Ella spent her weekends making us food for the week ahead. If she went on a road trip to Minneapolis with Clancy for the weekend, she premade homemade chili con carne and froze it so Tanya and I could heat it up in the microwave and scoop it onto slices of toast.

I loved being in charge. My mother would leave a hand-typed list of housekeeping rules taped to the wall before she left for a weekend getaway. The moment I heard the car leave the driveway, I flamboyantly ripped the paper in half in front of my sister's disapproving stare. (Tanya liked the rules.) I would turn up the stereo and dance around the living room, pretending we were going to live it up, which we never did. Although I did wear a groove into my mom's old vinyl record of The Troggs' "Wild Thing," I rarely invited friends to come over in case they did something crazy like carelessly setting a water glass down on the pristine coffee table without a coaster. A couple hours before Clancy and Ella's return, I would madly rush around vacuuming the carpets and scrubbing the crusted-over dishes lining the kitchen counters.

Once, Clancy had stuck a piece of invisible tape on a corner of the piano key lid before he and my mother left for a weekend trip to North Dakota. When they returned, he discovered I hadn't touched the piano because the tape was still intact. My mother got wildly upset at Clancy for tricking me. I was surprised that she stood up for me, even though it was true, I had lied. I was always trying to get out of practising.

When Ella was fighting with Clancy, a regular occurrence, they would head to the only bathroom upstairs and lock the door. We could hear their angry words trumpeting through the heating vents. Clancy was quite a bit younger, which annoyed my father. My father thought he was "big and fat and ugly." Regardless, my mother was pressuring Clancy to marry her. She told us she had visited a fortune teller who gave her the initials of her true love, C.A.R.: Clancy Arnold Robinson. We couldn't argue with that.

Clancy later told me that he felt he had been too young to have a ready-made family with two young daughters. My sister would sometimes call him Dad, but I was at an age where I resented him. I once wrote an essay called "Why I Hate Clancy." It included references to living in camp Sing Sing prison. I read this essay out loud to my mother and Clancy, which, I am sure, didn't improve our relationship. It was only after my mother died that he became an ally. He never married or had children of his own.

MY MOTHER was intent on finding a husband. At the time, I didn't understand why she was on a mission to be bound up with another man, especially after all the resentments she held against my father. Although I now have more of an understanding about how lonely a life can be with two little girls to tend to.

Eventually, Ella met someone who did want to marry her. His name was Ronald, and they met through the personal ads in the *Winnipeg Free Press*. Ronald and my mother were married within the year in a small ceremony in Hawaii. Ronald rented out his larger house across town and moved into our house on McAdam Avenue. They didn't bother to head up to the bathroom for their yelling matches. Something was always brewing between them.

"Whose scalloped potatoes do you like best?" my mother would ask at dinner.

I would thoughtfully taste each offering and say as diplomatically as I could, "Well, they're both very good."

"You see? Your daughter is an idiot. She can't tell that my scalloped potatoes are better," Ronald would say with a red face, his black hair stuck to the side of his sweating forehead.

"Don't you call my daughter an idiot!" my mother would scream in a high-pitched tone.

Tanya and I would get up in unison and leave them to it. We would head to the rec room in the basement, which my mother referred to as the dungeon, and finish our scalloped potatoes while watching TV. My mother rarely drank but somehow always ended up with men who did. To this day, I truly wonder if the whole world is made up of alcoholics.

One night I came home to find her in her pajamas scrubbing the carpet on her hands and knees. Ronald was vomiting in the basement bathroom. I had moved my pink futon into the basement bedroom, farther from the fray.

"Need any help?" I asked.

"No, I'm fine."

In a drunken stupor, Ronald had flushed his false teeth down the toilet. He covered his mouth whenever he talked for the week it took to get a new set of teeth.

IN WINNIPEG, we sometimes played on the curated grounds of the Rosh Pina synagogue, a short walk down our dead-end street. The neighbours' front lawns were closer though if we wanted to play sosketball, a game using rules from soccer, football, and basketball that often ended in bloodshed. We could tackle each other to get the soccer ball past the goalie standing between two shoes serving as goal posts set out at equal distances. This was the moment I realized boys might be different than girls. It wouldn't occur to me to run across the grass in a pair of clean socks. I watched in wonder as Robert Brick slid along the grass on his stomach, creating a muddy streak across his shirt front before he pulled it over his head, revealing a thin white torso. He turned it inside out and carried on. This behaviour fascinated me.

Most of the kids from our neighbourhood went to private Jewish school. Robert began training for his bar mitzvah when he was twelve. He had to recite passages from the *Torah*, entirely in Hebrew. Robert's bar mitzvah was held at the Rosh Pina synagogue when he turned thirteen. I sat in the audience, worrying not only about how frizzy my hair was that day, but I was equally anxious about Robert's propensity to stutter. I desperately hoped he could recite his prayers without stumbling on the words. I was in love. Sadly, it was not reciprocated. It could have been my mouthful of braces, or my unruly hair, or the fact that whenever he drove by on his ten-speed bicycle, with his dark hair falling rakishly across his eyes, I called out, fluttering my freshly painted nails from atop my mother's VW Rabbit, blowing bubbles like smoke signals.

I was one of the few non-Jews in the neighbourhood. Robert and his friend Jeffrey Greenburg concluded I was one quarter Jewish because Jewishness is determined by your mother's family tree, and my mother's mother, Big Baba had only married a Jew. Also, my mother was the only divorced woman on our block. Consequently, I had to prove I was fun and smart enough to be in their company, that public school was not a complete bust. When I was in Grade 2, we held a reading contest on Jeffrey's front lawn. Lucky for me, reading was my strong suit.

I attended Seven Oaks Elementary across the back lane. I could sleep in, down a glass of milk, and sprint down the block in my bell-bottom pants and still make it in time to stand in line to sing "O Canada" and recite the Lord's Prayer. *Our father who art in heaven, hallowed be thy name.*

Our principal, Mrs. Stewart, was terrifying. If you didn't know your times tables, you ended up in the special class where boys slouched in their chairs, inking designs on their jeans or hands when they thought no one was looking. As if this wasn't trying enough, our house was not in the school district and so attending was grounds for expulsion. My mother didn't follow these kinds of rules. Why go to school across town when there was one a short walk across the back lane? We used Big Baba's mailing address to enroll, but the situation gave me nightmares for six years. In an attempt to save on child care costs, my mother tried to enroll Tanya in Grade 1 a year early. I shifted guiltily in the chair in Mrs. Stewart's office, my face flushed with worry as my mother easily lied to my principal. She pretended Tanya was six, but Mrs. Stewart was no fool. She could tell she was too young by her lisp.

When I was caught for lying (again) about how long I had practised the piano (zero), I was banished to my room. I perched my elbows on my windowsill and listened with a breaking heart to the gang, including my beloved Robert, playing hide-and-seek until the mosquitoes drove them indoors. Although I loved nature, I did not know much about the local flora and fauna. I knew there were sparrows and robins in the neighbourhood, but when I found a snowy owl, stiff from the cold, lying on a crust of snow underneath the pine tree on our front lawn, I knew just how much I didn't know. There were trees with needles and trees with leaves; lilac bushes that were white, purple, and plum-coloured; and blue jays that dive-bombed my pigtailed head.

I was obsessed with capturing a bird. They were everywhere, pecking in the dirt, feathers so close I was sure I could trap one. I spent the long, hot summer days wandering the dusty boulevards of our short street or poking around the grounds of the Rosh Pina. If I saw a bird, I would stand completely still, skills gleaned from pretending I was a mannequin in the window at Zayda's shop. I was hoping to take it by surprise.

One day a cranky baby bird flew at me, and I reached out and caught it in my hands. I panicked when I felt the blue jay squirming between my sweaty palms. I hurried home with my captive held tight. Clancy's brother, Randy, was fixing his car in the driveway. He told me I shouldn't mess with nature; its mother was probably looking for it. I should take the baby bird back to the tree where I had found it. I was mortified. I ran back toward the Rosh Pina grounds with tears in my eyes, but the little bird got loose and flew off halfway down our block. Had I destroyed its only chance for survival?

In Grade 12, Robert finally took an interest in me and asked me to prom. By this time, I had scads of boyfriends and Robert no longer met my criteria as a love interest. He was too scrawny, and his stutter no longer made my heart clench. I borrowed my mother's black silk pantsuit with padded shoulders; I was a chunky Madonna or a member of the English new wave band, A Flock of Seagulls.

It was 1984. Every high school in Winnipeg held their graduation dinner and dance at the Fort Garry Hotel (where Big Baba once worked in the cafeteria). I spent the evening dancing with Robert's friend, Steve, while his date sat unhappily in a corner next to Robert watching us kick up our heels to Nena's "99 Luftballons" and Cyndi Lauper's "Girls Just Want to Have Fun," the soundtrack to my youth.

I HAD another fight with Ronald and my mother, so I knew it was time to go out on my own. I answered an ad to share an apartment within walking distance to the University of Winnipeg, where I had been accepted. I signed up for everything from physical anthropology to aerial photography to French Language Skills. I didn't have a clue what I was doing there; didn't have any plans.

My new roommate, Martin, was also attending university. His parents owned a suite in an old, converted heritage house.

I discovered Little Baba had worked in the very same house as a maid when she was young, cleaning up after a doctor and his family. I imagined my bedroom was once a pantry—it was long and narrow, the walls painted a vibrant peach. The bathroom had a clawfoot tub with a window permanently stuck open. Snowflakes flew into my hair as I heated my body in the bathwater every night. The walls of the living room had bookshelves lined with novels that I had never heard of. I was compelled to pluck the dusty classics off the shelves to read instead of opening my textbooks. Three hours would fly by, and I hadn't studied at all. It was from these crowded bookshelves that I discovered authors like Capote, Fitzgerald, Steinbeck, and Harper Lee.

I was exhausted from working nights, so Little Baba took it upon herself to call me every morning. I awoke to her voice echoing through the house, amplified by the answering machine.

"Margot, time to get up! Margot? Are you there? Oh, I hate these things . . ."

It felt wonderful to know someone cared enough to call you once a day. I was so distracted by my own busy life that I wasn't aware what was going on back at home. I rarely saw my mother because we were still fighting. I was still bitter about the time Ronald had called the police on me for "breaking and entering." In reality, I was permitted into the house by his son who was house-sitting while they were in Hawaii. I used a screwdriver to jimmy open the basement lock to take back the pink futon that I had paid for. Ronald and my mother were holding my furniture hostage to put pressure on my father to pay alimony.

I should have been suspicious when Ella volunteered to take me to my driver's test. (I was a later bloomer.) She walked stooped over like she was a hundred years old and had a bad back. When I asked her what was wrong, she was vague, mumbled something about a little operation. It didn't occur to me that it could be something serious.

I SOON realized that working full time until after midnight and attending early morning classes was not sustainable. I stumbled into classes and wrote my notes with my eyes closed. When I took my pages home to study, I discovered they were illegible. As a result, my marks were poor. So, I returned home. Tanya was glad I was back.

I WOKE from a dead sleep in the middle of the night to find my mother lying in the hallway, clutching the carpet in pain. She was waiting for Ronald to get dressed to take her to the emergency room. I ran upstairs to get her warm fuzzy socks, then down again to pull them over the green veins of her pale white feet. She smiled weakly and thanked me. This reversal of roles was deeply unsettling.

When she returned, she lay in her double bed all day, recovering from the operation. Her newfound interest in the afterlife and a book called *Life after Life* by Raymond Moodie were worrying. I read it late into the night. It contained stories of people's near-death experiences and accounts of what they saw, including the proverbial light at the end of the tunnel, beacons calling their souls back to earth. Uncle Victor's wife, my auntie Maria, had just been diagnosed with cancer, so the choice of my mother's bedside material seemed logical.

Within a few days, a life insurance officer came by to sign my mother up for a plan. She was so weak she had to sit in the living room under a blanket. I feared Ronald had pressured her to pretend she wasn't ill in order to get life insurance. Maybe she was worried about my sister and me. Maybe Ronald was concerned we might contest the house, and he would have to move back to his own across town?

Eventually, she couldn't conceal the truth any longer. My mother had ovarian cancer. It spread quickly. It got so bad she couldn't eat except tiny bits of food pierced on toothpicks.

She set up camp on the living room sofa, underneath her wall of framed art prints.

When one of her friends dropped by to visit, my mother joked, "I've got one foot in the grave and another on a banana peel."

I was scheduled to leave for Whistler, British Columbia, the following week to look for work in the mountains. I asked my mother if I should stay and she said, "What are you going to do? Sit around and wait for me to die?"

And so I left.

AFTER ONLY a few months in Whistler, my sister tracked me down through a co-worker at Blackcomb Mountain, I was working in the basement behind the ski check and the lost and found. I was surprised to find the young man standing nervously at the door of the house I rented with seventeen other people. No one had cell phones back then; we didn't have a land line. I was to call my sister right away. It was an emergency. Tanya must have telephoned my employers, who sent someone to find me. I was impressed.

When I called her back from the pay phone down the street, Tanya demanded I get home right away. Mom was dying. I gave notice to my two jobs (I was also waitressing nights at the Savage Beagle), packed up, left the boarding-house, and returned to Winnipeg. From the airport, I headed straight to my friend Laurie's apartment. She kindly offered me her black leather couch. I was still not on great terms with Ronald and didn't feel comfortable going "home."

Late one night, the phone rang, and I got the news that my mother had died. I have always regretted that I wasn't by her side.

I RETURNED to the house on McAdam Avenue to be a support for Tanya, but the tension was unbearable with Ronald, so Tanya and I moved in with Big Baba until we could figure out our next steps. Tanya was still in high school, and I had finally completed my university degree, but I felt like I had learned nothing. I was desperate to escape Winnipeg but felt responsible for my sister. I wanted to be there for Tanya (at the very least) while she finished high school.

AFTER A long court battle with Ronald, my sister and I lost the family home. My sister got a settlement of $5,000 (she generously gave me half). We also inherited a handful of my mother's jars of dill pickles. It is an odd feeling to be fed by your mother even after her death.

SPICY FERMENTED PINEAPPLE TEPACHE

This recipe is inspired by a Mexican recipe for a refreshing, fermented, zingy pineapple drink called tepache. It was traditionally made with corn but is now often made with pineapple (skin and all!), cinnamon, star anise, or cloves. We skip these spices and instead enjoy the addition of fresh unpeeled ginger and spicy Thai peppers. This zesty drink is quick and easy to make and is really good for you. If you can, use the whole pieces of organic pineapple and not just the rinds. Don't wash the pineapple, if you dare, to keep all the good bacteria that kickstarts the fermentation process. Feel free to cut down on the number of hot peppers or, for a milder taste, you can omit them entirely. This recipe works best when the tepache is stored at warm room temperature (between 16 and 29°C) to ferment the fruit properly. You will need a 1-gallon glass jar covered with a coffee filter and rubber band, or a flat lid to allow gasses to release during fermentation.

1 cup brown sugar

1 whole well-ripened
organic pineapple
(top removed, leave
skin on)

½ cup fresh ginger, skin
on, roughly chopped

1–2 Thai chili peppers,
cut into rough pieces
(optional)

1 gallon water (Use only
fresh distilled or
filtered water. Do not
use chlorinated water.)

Pour enough room temperature water into the bottom of the glass jar and stir well to dissolve brown sugar. Fill the jar with the roughly chopped unpeeled pineapple chunks, ginger pieces and 1 or 2 hot peppers.

Fill up the jar with water, make sure to cover your fruit with fluid. Cover the jar with a coffee filter or cheese cloth and seal with a rubber band, and set the jar on the kitchen counter. Let the tepache sit at room temperature for up to 3 days or more depending on the weather. If it is hot, fermentation occurs faster. Shake or stir the liquid once a day. Taste the tepache after a couple of days. How does it taste? If it is too sweet, the fermentation process is not complete. If it ferments too long, it will have a sour taste and may turn to vinegar. Once you reach the desired taste, strain the liquid and serve cold.

Place the rest of your tepache in the refrigerator to stop fermentation. Good news: You may reuse the fermented pineapple to make more tepache. Add another cup of brown sugar into filtered water and stir to dissolve. Pour over the well-fermented fruit and top up with more water. Wait a day or two. This batch will ferment faster, so taste test it to make sure it doesn't turn to vinegar. Serve over ice on a hot summer day.

CAREFUL OF
THE BONES

GROWING UP in Winnipeg, where the winters have been recorded as colder than Siberia, I had an unnatural fear of frostbite. I was afraid of everything as a child—swimming in the deep end of the pool, the clown painting on the wall in the basement, cats in heat. I didn't learn how to ride a bike until I was ten. I was also afraid of choking on the pale, sharp bones in fish.

"Careful of the bones!" my mother warned me.

Fear had held me back as long as I could remember, so it took no small amount of pluck to do what I did next.

On one of the bulletin boards at the university, when I had been studying for my degree, I had discovered an ad that read: TREE PLANTERS WANTED IN NORTHERN BC. I furtively ripped off the little tab of paper with the number on it and stuffed it into my pocket.

It was a dark winter day when I pulled out the scrunched up piece of paper. I sat on my Russian baba's plush red velvet couch and dialed the number. Carol, the crew boss of the planting company Mudslide, spent forty-five minutes drilling me, while I did my best to convince her I was the perfect person for the job. I fidgeted with the gold tassels on my grandmother's lamp, the fringe on a shade the shape of a Spanish tango dancer.

Carol tried to warn me of the hardships, "It's physically demanding. You need to be on your feet for ten hours a day."

I told her it sounded wonderful. I got the job.

I started in the middle of April 1990. Even though I had earned a degree in environmental studies, I didn't know how to find a job in my field. I had no clue where to start looking. At school, I had studied weather patterns like jet streams, about which I wrote an incredibly long meandering essay on my final exam, and still didn't achieve high marks. But it was a Theory in Philosophy class that had really sparked my interest when we learned about morality. I picked up the phrase "victim of the sensual pleasures." I would pull this out at parties to impress my friends, while we were hot-knifing hash over someone's electric stove. I would put the back of my hand to my forehead and say, "Oh, I can't help myself. I am a victim of the sensual pleasures."

I had a lucrative job at a popular bar called the Marble Club. I had served Sex on the Beach and Slippery Nipples cocktails in a smokey room until 2 AM. I made enough tips in one month to pay for a whole year's tuition and was even able to pay for a backpacking trip to Europe one summer. I went out dancing to the same kinds of clubs on my nights off, wearing pink-fringed cowboy boots. The long strings of white plastic pearls wound attractively (I thought) around my wrists and ankles jingled with each of my steps. I wore a black lacy bra overtop of my T-shirt; I desperately wanted to look like Madonna. When drunk enough, I would admit out loud that I really wanted to live on a farm and make my own soap.

My friends would look at me incredulously and laugh it off, but deep down I craved a rugged life. I was drawn to people who found solace in the outdoors, who took joy in a sky crowded with stars.

In 1990, Tanya and I were still living with Big Baba. We had my zayda's funeral the same winter that we buried my mother. We couldn't bear to live in the same house with Ronald. Our biological father lived in Edmonton. It was hard to keep up with where he was with his addictions. Besides, I had my own issues.

I shared my baba's large bedroom with Tanya while Big Baba moved into the smaller guest room down the hall. Every night we would fall asleep on the waterbed, the smell of mothballs a strange sensory accompaniment to the voice of Daniel Lanois singing soulful French songs on a cassette. To cheer ourselves up, we fantasized about eventually getting an apartment together and adopting a kitten; I would support Tanya with tips while she finished high school. We had to hang onto the wooden sides of the bed to keep our bodies from rolling into each other. We would call the kitten Baroness Gaby von Bag of Boo, from a book of odd names we found at the library.

I said goodbye to my sister on a cool day in April, promising to return with bags of money. After a three-day, bone-rattling bus trip across the country, I arrived at the parking lot in Prince George, my huge backpack at my feet with sand stuck in the creases from a trip to Europe the summer before. I tried to look nonchalant as I cast glances at the odd assortment of people waiting with me. It was mostly men in work boots with grey socks folded over the tops. It was a style that I would soon mimic.

We piled into trucks called Crummies and were driven to a logging camp about thirteen kilometres away. I was mesmerized by the BC landscape. The trees were taller, the flowers more vibrant than back home in Winnipeg. The clouds touched down on the curve of the highway, our truck hurtling through the layers of the stratosphere.

We were assigned small rooms with army-style cots. My roommate was a brunette named Desiree. Camp cost eighteen dollars a day and included three huge meals.

Tree planters were a different breed of people. The crew featured many French Canadians, swarthy men in red bandanas with strong jawlines. They rolled their own cigarettes and played Hacky Sack with tiny colourful bean bags. Some carried guitars and sang songs around the campfire. I was drawn to them, and then to one in particular.

On the first day, Carol strapped a white vinyl planting bag onto my shoulders and showed me how to use the shovel I had purchased the day before. I wore my new pair of heavy-duty cork boots with metal spikes on the bottoms that allowed me to jump from log to log and get a grip up the steep side of the mountain.

All the newbies went with Carol. She drove us up to a planting or "cut block"—a vast tract of land that had been logged, with debris burned into an impenetrable layer. This was called slash-and-burn. We were instructed to line our bags with moss to keep the tree seedlings cool. We were told to walk in rhythm: *walk walk walk, screef screef.* Screefing was the act of digging the soft debris or "duff" until actual soil was found. Each planter then sliced the earth with their shovel, plopped in the tree, and stomped down the hole. We were expected to repeat this until they picked us up eight hours later. I was a slow learner.

We were paid eighteen cents for every tree planted. I would have to plant a lot of trees to cover camp costs and pay for my equipment. Some days I only planted three hundred trees, despite trying hard. It took me a long time to get up to eight hundred trees, but I was never a "high baller," planting over a thousand trees a day. I was too careful, too worried my little trees would get kinked "J-roots" if I didn't tend to them. This was not a good mindset for making money.

In the mornings I woke up with my hands clenched, the bones bruised. This we jokingly called the planter's claw, the painful result of clutching the shovel's wooden handle all day.

Before heading out, I ate a bowlful of oatmeal with sweet, canned peaches and packed a lunch from a table piled high with fixings. I was vegetarian at the time, so I ate hummus sandwiches with pickles, on the move, to escape the relentless mobs of mosquitoes.

At the cut block, I was alone. I breathed in the cool morning air. I clipped my yellow Sony Walkman to my planting bag, put in my earphones, and turned up Vivaldi's "The Four Seasons." The energetic sawing of the violins seemed like the perfect background for striding over logs and planting trees. Each day I felt stronger. I savoured the isolation. I laughed out loud when a moose thundered past where I stood, too stunned to move, my sandwich in mid-air. Each night we were picked up and returned to the logging camp for a shower and dinner. There was one member of the crew, a tall stern-faced male who would jog back to camp from the planting block for "extra" exercise. I watched him through the dirty, streaked truck window, wondering if he was an alien. I was beyond exhausted from so much fresh air. I could hardly keep my eyes open. At 8 PM, I crawled into my sleeping bag, too tired to think about my mother's death or Tanya waiting at home.

Slowly, I got to know the crew and all their foibles, particularly the men. A tall French Canadian ate mushrooms, hoping for a psychedelic experience, but instead spent the day vomiting. Many people were fresh out of jail. Clearly, they would take anyone.

Tomas was a small, muscular Hungarian who was released from jail only to learn that he had cancer. His face was round and childlike, and he would sometimes sing and dance until he passed out. Sometimes he was unable to get up for work. One morning we found him asleep on the old truck bench we had pulled up as seating around the campfire. He had wet himself. However, he had found a tribe of caring people in our unlikely assortment. He had bad eyesight and no money for glasses, so the crew boss had to mark his whole section of the cut block with neon yellow flagging tape to help him space his trees properly. His gentle nature compelled people to protect him.

One of our crew bosses chewed his arms due to an anxious condition, but he played the flute beautifully. One of the attractive girls on the crew, who juggled batons of fire, was sleeping with him. A couple of clean-cut preppies, Dave (the cuter one) said, "When we signed up for this job, we imagined a long golf course with a flat green lawn. I didn't think I would be hanging off a mountain trying to dig down a foot to make a lousy eighteen cents a tree."

I spent a lot of time with Dave and his friend Aaron because they reminded me of boys in Winnipeg. Sometimes we would drive to a sports bar to eat potato skins smothered in cheese and complain over sweating pints of beer.

Secretly, I felt tougher than them.

We all had copies of *Screef Magazine*, which held contests inviting us to enter our best bear stories for fifty dollars. At the back of the magazine, there was a list of all the planting companies listed in alphabetical order: Apex, Evergreen, Golden Raven Green Trees, Nechako, Nu Growth, Hawkeye, Roots, Silvaram, Silverado, Summit, and Zanzibar to name a few. Most were run out of Prince George. The company I was working for, Mudslide, was quite large and well run, except for the time a couple of English girls were left on the planting block with a grizzly. No one noticed they were missing until a few hours after dinner. We drove back to the planting block and were relieved to find them hiding under a tarp, chain-smoking rolled cigarettes and singing.

Back at camp, someone had stolen the partition from the shower tent so that the male tree planters could ogle the young girls' bodies while they washed away the day's layers of dirt. It didn't bother me as I loved to strip off my shirt and plant topless on a hot day. Why couldn't I take off my shirt, like any man could? I relished the feel of the mountain breeze on my damp skin. I was pulsing with life. I was adventurous and free with my body and wanted to reinvent myself. I didn't want to be the sad girl whose mom had just died of cancer.

At the end of a long day of planting, we waited in line for our turn in the shower. That day, I noticed one of the male planters named Rick was fishing for a scrap of muddy soap that someone had dropped beneath the slats of wood. I was disgusted, casting a sideways glance at his pale naked backside. He had wide, thick shoulders and a long white back. Years later we would tell our daughters this story around the dinner table and laugh. He later admitted that he always made sure to wait in line at the wash tent when he knew I was going to be there. Rick did not look like someone who would change my life. He drove an orange VW van with a picture of Sid Vicious taped to the window.

"This is my off season," he explained. "I'm an urchin diver." Before I met Rick, I had no idea what an urchin diver did. He had a little kitten the colour of toffee that climbed up his arm as he drove. He called it Screefer.

Rick had orange curly hair that clashed with the turquoise Hawaiian shirt he wore every day. Rick had an athlete's job; he lived in his body, so different from any of the pale Winnipeg boys I knew who drank lite beer and had studied next to me at the library. They had thin, weak arms and were persnickety. Rick's stories always involved reaching for wild things with his muscly arms.

"I was in this Zodiac, on the Athabasca River," he told me one night over a pitcher of cheap draft beer. "This bear swam by us, so I drove right up to it and grabbed its fur."

"You what?"

"It's rage was so huge, I thought it was going to land in the boat." He laughed.

If my mother had been alive to meet him, I knew she wouldn't approve—someone who lived in motels between dive jobs.

Rick later admitted his mother may not have liked the fact that I was Jewish, though that was part of what drew him to me. Sadly, I wasn't as Jewish as he had hoped. Here I was trying my hardest to not be my parents, but like they had been, I was drawn to someone whom my parents wouldn't approve of.

One afternoon Rick and I were dropped off at the edge of a gravel logging road. We peered over the slash-and-burn, plotting our best route for the remainder of our trees. It was one o'clock, and I had already put in five hours. Rick invited me to join him for a cigarette. My arms felt like rubber, so I agreed to stop for a rest. He took a photo of me in my tree planter's attire: cargo shorts over black tights, long grey socks pulled up to where the red stipe reached mid-calf. Baby trees were sticking straight out of my planting bags that hung heavy on my hips. My foot rested on the edge of my planting shovel. I wanted him to capture the snow-capped mountains in the distance to show Tanya back home.

Afterward, as we sat on the ground, Rick told me a story of how one day when he came back from a diving trip, he had found a naked man hiding in his closet. His girlfriend had the bed covers up to her chin and looked upset because she was caught.

"That's crazy! Who would do that to someone?" I cast my eyes to the ground, remembering the debauchery that had occurred on the Greek islands during my trip to Europe the summer before, paid for by two of my waitress gigs. At the time, I had a boyfriend waiting for me back home in Winnipeg that I conveniently forgot about.

I rolled my shoulders and felt the warmth of the sun on my back, as Rick and I sat quietly, lost in our own thoughts. I took a drag from my rolled cigarette and when I had smoked most of it, I used it to light another one, a useful trick I had picked up for those times when you are low on matches. I was in no hurry to go back to work on this section of hillside. The steep incline made my knees hurt. It felt good to sit and talk about Rick's problems, which forced me to not think about my own.

Rick told me his father had died of cancer years before. His mother still lived in Fort McMurray. She took on boarders to keep her company. He told me that he knew his parents had loved each other very much.

"How did you know?" I asked, ever curious about long-lasting love.

"I just did," he said in a way that made me believe him.

AFTER THE spring plant, we had a short break and then we moved to a site near McBride, BC, for the summer plant. I pitched my tent on the side of a hill away from everyone, enjoying the feeling of isolation. Another woman took out the seat of her VW to sleep comfortably with her dog. She loaned me books by Leon Rooke. I read *Shakespeare's Dog* and *Fat Woman* at night by flashlight.

I wrote at night while hunched in my sleeping bag with damp tent walls sagging toward me. Here is an excerpt from my diary: *July 23, Raining hard—Looking out over the trees, still light out—purple tall fleurs—white itty-bitty ones and my old rotten log that is my white picket fence in front of my Eureka home. I wish someone was in here with me . . .*

For three days it rained solid. Rick was snug and dry in his VW. He invited me to bring my sleeping bag to camp out in his van but I declined. One night during a particularly heavy rainstorm, when water began to leak through the top of my tent, I had the brain wave to take off all my clothes to keep them from getting wet. I unzipped the tent and climbed outside to fasten a black garbage bag over the saturated roof of my Eureka tent. When I stepped outside, the smell of wet earth filled my nose. I felt a moment of joy then, as the rain pelted my bare skin. Back inside, I took a towel and dried myself off and crawled back into my warm sleeping bag. I slept contentedly through the rest of the night.

AFTER THE summer plant was finished, Rick offered to drive me to Edmonton to visit my father, Frank. He said, "No problem. Edmonton's not too far out of my way to Mexico."

He drove me to my father's apartment, and he slept in his van in the parking lot next to the dumpster out back. The next night we joined my father for dinner at the Rose Bowl Pizza restaurant down the road, my father's favourite hangout. I equated my father with short visits. After the divorce, Tanya and I stayed with Dad on weekends as part of the divorce agreement, until he moved to Edmonton. I always thought he moved far away to drink himself into oblivion without scrutiny from his family. He was generous when I visited him. He always insisted he pay for our meals out. I knew he was back to drinking—I could hardly stand to see the way he drank cheap rye whiskey, until his words slurred, and his face went slack and stupid. I was grateful for the distraction of Rick and his friend Kiwi who came all the way from New Zealand to plant trees in BC. The next morning, we visited Whyte Avenue, where I suggested Rick get a haircut, and he obeyed.

Were we unconsciously falling into invisible roles? I now wonder. Was I playing the role of the wife, telling her "husband" what to do? I have a photo of Rick from that day. He sports his new haircut as he stands next to his friend Kiwi in front of his orange vw van. His kitten, Screefer, is held in front of him, like he is offering it up to me. Later, I would learn it was his nature to rescue. He would bring home arthritic kittens and pathetic dogs I would be left in charge of, along with squalling children, while he was away diving.

Rick wrote me a series of rude postcards from his road trip to Baja California Peninsula with Kiwi. He wrote out the rude lines of an April Wine song, code for a swear word. This daring gesture pleased me (oddly) because Rick knew I was now staying at my baba's. I still have the battered postcards in a box somewhere, as proof of our courtship.

When I returned to Winnipeg, I sported a T-shirt that read: *Pardon me thou bleeding piece of earth, that I am meek and gentle with these butchers.* My sister had poison ivy, thanks to being a camp counsellor, so I made her wrap herself in a sheet before we inevitably touched in the dent of the waterbed. We needed our own apartment and separate beds. I got a job at the busy bar at the restaurant Grapes on Main to add to my savings, and we made the move.

WINNIPEG WAS getting too small for me. I felt like I had slept with everyone in the city by the time I was twenty-three. Perhaps this was what my mother meant when she accused me of being just like my father. Although this experience came in handy when I was looking for an apartment to rent without any references. An old flame, Les Hardman, who was the caretaker of a building in downtown Winnipeg told me a basement suite was available in a red brick three-storey walk-up. It had thin hardwood plank floors, a clawfoot tub, and steam radiators. Tanya and I loved it.

We went to a second-hand store and selected an over-stuffed flower-patterned couch. Ronald didn't want to let

Tanya have her bedroom furniture until it went through the lawyers. So, for the first couple of months, Tanya slept next to me on my pink futon. When her furniture arrived, we discovered we didn't like having a wall between us. We had become accustomed to late-night chats, whispering under the covers about our days' events as we drifted off to sleep.

As promised, we went to the SPCA and picked up a little black and white kitten. When we got it home, it appeared there was something wrong with it. It was prone to attacking, clamped down hard on our hands, drew blood. He was a killer at heart, and so we ironically named him Petunia. Soon the neighbours hated us because the kitten stalked and killed baby bunnies. I put a little bell around his murderous neck, but it didn't help. His innate nature was to hunt. We were a bit frightened of him, but we had made a commitment to love him. We decided to pick up another cat to keep him company, hoping it would help or distract him from his mood swings. We decided on a female tortoise shell. We had decided on her name months ago during out late night chats. We called her Baroness Gaby Von Bag of Boo, Kitty boo for short.

Tanya and I settled into a rhythm. The apartment was a long drive from Tanya's high school across town, so my mother's old boyfriend, Clancy, let us borrow his car. The only problem with having a car in downtown Winnipeg was that we had no parking spot. After working until 2 AM, I set my alarm, stuffed my bare feet into snow boots, and trudged through the slushy sidewalks before 10 AM to get the car. Bleary-eyed, I would drive the car around the block to erase the chalk marks on the tires so I wouldn't get a ticket. Sometimes I missed the alarm and did get a ticket.

This suite had other drawbacks. We caught a man peering through our bathroom window while we bathed, so when an apartment opened up on the third floor, we moved. We weren't the first on the list for the new apartment, but thanks to Les and our brief romantic past, we got first dibs. Besides, he was tired of getting late nights calls from us to chase away the Peeping Toms.

Clancy would often call and take me out to a place that served "the best fries in Winnipeg" or "burgers you just *had* to try." He almost always ended our conversations with "I should have married your mother." This was a reference to Ronald winning my mother's house in court after her death. Clancy hated that my sister and I were forced to move out and be on our own.

Out of the blue I got a call from Rick, who was still in Mexico. He said he wanted to buy me a plane ticket to fly down and join him. I asked my boss for a week off.

"He doesn't want to be your friend," my manager said. He didn't give me the time off, and I didn't accept Rick's offer.

I HAD promised my sister I would stay in Winnipeg with her for a year, even though I wanted to escape the city and all the misery it represented. I craved a fresh start. When Tanya was nearing her high school graduation, I found her a roommate and moved to Vancouver without much savings and no real plan.

I lived in a bachelor apartment off Robson. I shared the apartment with two other women, Erin and Diyah. Diyah was a waitress friend from Winnipeg, working at the Commodore Ballroom making killer tips, enough to go to Emily Carr University of Art + Design. My bedroom was a blow-up mattress on the floor of the dining nook. I was twenty-four years old and needed an extra job. During the day I was working full-time, ironically, at a career consulting firm as a receptionist, but I needed to increase my income.

I saw a Help Wanted sign in the darkened window of the Penthouse Nightclub, and like the opening scene from the TV sitcom *Alice*, I walked in and was hired on the spot. I would begin waitressing the following night.

The words "strip club" may bring to mind a smokey room with men dangling cigarettes from their lascivious lips, fogging up their glasses and fumbling hands beneath the tables. However, the luster of this place, if it had ever existed, was clearly long gone. Customers said clubs across town were much ritzier, but there were still plenty of men who populated the Penthouse, rundown or not. I tried to remain removed from the drama of the place. I reminded myself this was just a means to an end, to save for trips to Mexico, Central America—anywhere but here.

I liked to think of myself as a kind of cultural anthropologist, investigating each stripper's ingenuity. One dancer squirted paint on her body to create outlines of her breasts on posters she sold from the stage to a sea of reaching hands. She put herself through university this way. The owner, Danny, was young, handsome, and oddly down-to-earth. He was dating one of the strippers, he told everyone proudly with a wry smile, which seemed to imply they were just honest hard-working girls who know how to make a buck.

All the long shabby tables were occupied by prostitutes, mingling with the customers. Because I had never been in a strip club before, I thought this was ordinary practice. My female manager said we must treat the prostitutes with respect and refer to them as "ladies." During a shift, one of the ladies was yelling at a man, "Leave me alone! Quit bothering me!" She had a delicate nose, dyed blonde curls sprayed with too much hairspray, and deep crow's feet that made her look as if she hadn't had a good night's sleep in years. She spit at him.

He was one of her long-time clients and obsessed with her. He looked stricken by her words, as if he didn't understand their relationship was financial not romantic. The line between client and lover got easily blurred in such intimate work.

Alternatively, the women on stage had breasts that were impressive, perfect orbs with bright red nipples. Their youthful skin had no bulges; they were rosy powdered perfection. I felt ungainly and gnomish in the shadow of these women. My small but perky breasts had one wonky nipple, but I had a flat stomach and strong shapely arms. I had perfected a cringe-worthy party howl with hip gyrations that I would perform when warranted, but at the Penthouse, I chose to wear a thick black turtleneck rather than "show some skin." I was a different kind of working girl, but I also needed to make money in a world where men make the rules. At the end of a long shift, I just wanted to peel off my thick black stockings with a tiny hole in the toe and fall into bed with someone who would reach for me beneath the warm blankets.

On New Year's Eve, the club held a dinner without entertainment, so there were many disgruntled men wandering around in search of naked women and a grope during the countdown to midnight. Unsavory men, or drunk managers with boozy breath, tried to kiss unsuspecting waitresses or sip champagne from a sweaty stiletto. I took drink orders and gave the appearance of being too busy and kept my mouth away from probing tongues. I expertly held a tray over my head, filled with highball drinks clinking with ice cubes and red plastic straws. At the stroke of midnight, a small man, dressed in a tidy business suit, walked over and lifted up my shirt with the glee of a naughty schoolboy.

"Happy New Year!" he yelled.

I had my hands full and wasn't able to stop him.

Hence, the turtleneck and matching black skirt and stockings. My dark form waded through the underbrush of men's desires, passing out sweating glasses of sickly-sweet rye and coke, doubles tossed back by men whose eyes didn't leave the stage. I didn't want the men's gazes to glance my way and they rarely did. They couldn't keep their eyes off of those long legs in sparkly, spiked sandals pumping to the teasing lyrics of "U Can't Touch This" by MC Hammer. I had thick ankles and wore comfortable shoes. The men only glanced at me when I handed them their alcohol.

One night, I was approached by a young Indian couple, the woman in a sari and the man in a turban. They were with their elderly father who was "in need of a woman," the younger man told me. They looked nervous and explained they didn't know the system. Neither did I, but with an overpowering need to help them out, I went directly to the table of "ladies" and pointed out the man in need of their services. They laughed and declined. I felt ashamed for everyone, for the old, undesirable men and the young sex workers, for being a part of the money game myself. I told the threesome it was their night off, and they looked both confused and disappointed.

I rarely questioned the morality of prostitution or stripping because my father had been fond of exotic dancers. He was proud of the fact he had many strippers who were clients who took advantage of his private tax accounting service, "Because even strippers and hookers need to do their taxes," he would say. He was fat and balding, the same sort of clientele who thronged to the Penthouse every night and every day.

An even seedier section of the club, less obvious from the street, catered to men who couldn't wait until the evening to see naked women's bodies. One Sunday I took a shift at the day club for another waitress. Here, instead of a woman dancing onstage, a young girl danced in the middle of the room with chairs circling the dance floor. I thought she stripped inelegantly, judging her with ten years of snobbish ballet training giving me the ability to sniff out an amateur in an instant. She swiped a pair of glasses right off of an old man's face and proceeded to smudge the lenses with her nipples. She pranced with his glasses perched precariously on her fleshy breasts.

I made killer tips that rubbed the matches in my apron. The friction of walking back and forth through the crowds of men caused my apron to catch fire. When I smelled the smoke, I dumped the contents onto the bar and pounded at the wads of money with my bare hands. I had worked too hard to let two hundred dollars go up in flames. I laughed at the ridiculousness of it all. I wondered, *Was spontaneous combustion a real thing?*

I SURPRISED myself when I was compelled to contact Rick with the only phone number I had, for his mother, Louise, in Fort McMurray. The next month he called me from Victoria where he was living in a motel and diving around Sooke Harbour. We arranged a day when Rick would take the ferry over and I would pick him up from the bus depot in downtown Vancouver. I made him my specialty, fettucine alfredo with fake crab meat. (Prairie folk do not always think to buy fresh crab.) We drank wine and watched *Night of the Living Dead*. "*They're coming to get you, Barbara!*"

I kissed his soft lips, and soon he was coming every weekend to Vancouver, between dives off Vancouver Island. We made love to opera music in stolen moments of privacy in a bachelor apartment shared with my two roommates. We went out to restaurants on Robson, eating at two restaurants, if we couldn't choose one. For extra cash, I gave food demos at a grocery store, so Rick hung out in the condiment section waiting to take me out to eat afterward. Sometimes I met him at a hotel in Victoria if that was easier, joining him in a motel room, one bed covered with empty pizza boxes and empty matchboxes from the cigarettes Rick would smoke. The housekeepers refused to enter Rick's room, so I rolled up my sleeves and helped him clean up the debris.

AFTER RICK and I started dating I drove to Port Renfrew one weekend to see him with my roommate, Diyah. We booked a few days off from work and caught the ferry to Sidney, driving along Highway 14 past Mystic Beach to Port Renfrew, a town near the trailhead for the West Coast Trail. Rick was working near there, diving for purple urchins for an experimental fishery at the time in the Juan de Fuca Strait. We were travelling in Billie, a Toyota Tercel I had named after Billie Holiday, though the soundtrack to my life was more aptly Joe Jackson's album "Jumpin Jive." We sang along to his version of "Is You Is or Is You Ain't My Baby."

I let Diyah drive because the winding highway made me nervous, and it would have taken forever if I had puttered along at sixty kilometres an hour, clutching the steering wheel and deep breathing to calm myself. We drove past ancient forests and billowing storm clouds with growing excitement about our foray into the wilds of Vancouver Island. As I flipped the cassette to listen to the other side, we heard a loud rhythmic *swack,* like giants thumping heavy clubs, blow after blow. We pulled the car onto a side road to investigate and walked along a winding tree-lined path, following the sound.

When the trail opened up, the cool wind hit our faces. We saw the white foam of the ocean's waves, smashing onto the rocky shore. Mystery solved. Two girls from the prairies had failed to recognize the sound of the surf. In Manitoba you might hear the sound of a loon's high-pitched wail at sunset or the smack of a beaver's tail on the flat surface of a lake, but not this.

Diyah was applying to Emily Carr University to study photography, so we took the opportunity to take photos: me, naked on the beach, long hair draped languorously over the rugged bark of a fallen log.

An hour later, when we sashayed into Port Renfrew's only pub, our cheeks flushed red from the wind, the crowd seemed to part for us. The divers' heads turned towards us in unison like sunflowers to the sun. The wind through the door seemed to lift our hair and set it back in place like a ghostly hairdresser primping us for the night's escapades. We were two young women in city clothes who jangled as we walked to the bar, jewelry flashing like metal lures enticing the plentiful fish in the sea.

Within minutes we owned the place. We handed the bartender our tape of "Jumpin' Jive" and soon '40s swing hung in the smokey air.

We didn't buy a drink all night as the only women in the joint. Our lights shone brighter than Jesus's gold halo in the paintings Little Baba was so fond of. We leaned over the pool table, making bad shots with cues propped inexpertly between our long fingers. The bar's walls were covered with bills sporting the scrawls of names and boats. The fishermen were tall and broad-shouldered, clad in thick grey sweaters rolled up to their elbows, dirt-caked rubber boots leaving a trail by their bar stools. Their dark eyes flashed as they doled out twenties. They were paid in cash at the end of each workday, which was then siphoned back to the hotel each night—not a great savings plan.

Rick always stood out with his head of thick orange curls and wide shoulders. He was fond of showing off his muscles, flexing them for me. He was also proud to have been the catalyst, enticing two beautiful girls to join his diving friends, in their insular world that normally consisted of only male companionship. He leaned in close, listening attentively as we laughed and recounted our tale of the strange sounds on the side of the road—how foolish we were to not know that the ocean wasn't as quiet as the lakes back home in Manitoba. We couldn't stop smiling at each other. My face hurt from so much laughter.

At the end of the night, after many Rusty Nail drinks, we stumbled up the stairs to the motel room above the pub. Diyah took one bed and I took the other. Rick gallantly fell asleep on the hard floor between us.

In the middle of the night Diyah said, "Margot! Rick's snoring. Make him stop."

I smacked Rick on the shoulder, but he only grunted, turned over, and continued snoring.

The reading lamp rattled in sync with each noisy breath.

THE NEXT "blow day," a day too windy to work, the men escorted us to Botanical Beach to explore the tidal pools. We didn't have proper shoes, so the men rooted around in the back of their pickup trucks and under the seats to supply us with footwear to navigate the pools, brimming with sea life. Rick grazed the tip of my finger along the sticky tentacles of an anemone so that it curled inward. I was fascinated.

The next day Rick and the other divers had to work so Diyah and I went spelunking in a nearby cave. We climbed over slippery rocks in dark caverns while the men dove deep underwater collecting urchins in seas called the Graveyard of the Pacific for the wild storms that took ships down. I could feel myself being pulled, too. It was impossible to fight the forces that were dragging me to its depths.

When we said goodbye in the parking lot, Rick handed me a hundred dollars to pay for the ferry and gas. I took it, like I was already practising for my role as a fishwife with her hand out on payday.

WHEN WE got back to the city, Diyah and I decided to join a women's operatic choir. On our first day of rehearsals, we learned that it would cost over $100 each for sheet music and administrative fees. We were commiserating over a glass of wine at a small bar on Robson when two older men joined us at our table.

After we recounted our story, one of the men said, "You must not be disappointed. Take this money for the choir and a cab ride home. My name is Prince something-something-something." He handed us two crisp $100 bills and an extra twenty for the fare.

We hadn't even needed Joe Jackson, and this was no Moe. Yet, all I could think of was Rick, far away and under the water, tugging on the lures around my wrist.

It was on one of these visits to Victoria that I knew I was in love. Rick took me out on the dive boat called *The Seeker* and laughed and pointed at a startled duck skimming the water with its wings. This was where I fell in love, out on the ocean on a cramped aluminum boat on a clear sunny day.

Later when he asked me to go to Mexico with him, I said yes. I was motivated to get to a beach where I could peel off my clothes and let the sand warm my body after playing in the surf all day.

WE DRANK three dollar bottles of Gato Negro wine, holed up in cheap motel rooms without screens, never leaving our hot room until hunger forced us out into the warm night air, pulsing with the sound of cicadas.

I could hear land crabs scrabbling at the walls, the colourful *tajalines* who were on a mission to get to the beach to lay their eggs. There was no stopping them. They had such a powerful drive to reproduce. They were everywhere, outside the restaurant patios we frequented at night, and I would watch fascinated as local women took brooms and thwacked the crabs off the walls of the deck where we ate spicy rice and beans and drank cheap bottles of Mexican beer. I cringed when I heard the hard shells of those crabs being crushed under the wheels of cars.

If the weather was not perfect, we would stay indoors. I would lie with one leg off the edge of the bed, angling myself so that I didn't miss a whisper of the breeze. Rick patiently taught me complicated sailor's knots with a shoelace tied to a wooden chair, which I promptly forgot after each lesson.

Sometimes we camped out in hammocks on the beach at Playa Zipolite so Rick could body surf in the huge waves. I was too scared of the undertow especially after discovering Zipolite comes from the Nahuatl word *sipolitlan* or *zipotli*, meaning "bumpy place" or "place of continuous bumps or hills." However, some claim the name means "beach of the dead" because of the dangerous underwater currents.

Round donut-shaped life preservers were placed strategically along the length of the beach. I witnessed a rescue the first day we arrived. A middle-aged tourist was slowly getting pulled out to sea and was flailing as people stood up and pointed toward him. A few cabana owners hesitantly walked toward their life preservers and glanced at each other as if to say, "Hey, isn't it your turn to rescue the stupid gringo this time? I did it yesterday."

Eventually, the man managed to ride a wave, and everyone stared as he staggered back to shore. Rick assured me that the waves come in sets of seven and with practice and counting you could ride the last and largest one safely to the shallows.

One day while Rick took his afternoon siesta, I took a refreshing swim in the cool waters. Eventually, the undertow managed to pull me out, and people stood up and pointed toward *me*. I was doubly ashamed because I was a *naked* dumb gringo getting washed out to sea. I looked frantically at Rick, who was rocking obliviously in his hammock. I could tell no one felt like rescuing me. I desperately counted the waves, and finally I felt my feet hit the sandy bottom. I walked on shaky legs to my towel, wrapped it around me, and hit Rick on the shoulders with my cold, wet hands. "Tomorrow we are leaving this horrible beach of death!"

We heard that you could hike to a remote beach to a place where there were no cabanas and no people, if you followed the waterline. So we left early the next morning to beat the heat. When the going got rough, we had to time the waves so we wouldn't get thrashed against the rocky shore. Rick would go first and count for me: "One, two, three, go!" Soon, we were on paths winding steeply uphill, and the pounding sun was unbearable. We had been walking for at least four hours.

. A group of Mexican children met us on the path, and with our meagre Spanish we managed to ask them if there was anywhere to get food. They led us to a small turquoise shack on an isolated beach. Underneath a tin roof was one solitary picnic table. A middle-aged Mexican woman came out to take our order. We ordered Coke, and the cold liquid sliding down my parched throat was almost sensual. Only one meal was on offer: a *pescado* (fish) dinner for 17,000 pesos. To keep on budget, we ordered one. While we waited, we took in the rocks and the hill behind us and the ocean stretching before us, the flashing silver waves and the clear blue skies. Eventually, side dishes of rice and beans, fresh salsas, and green sauce arrived. Out came a platter of perfectly grilled fish, the scent of cumin, fresh coriander, and hot lime wafting in the cool breeze. Rick swooned—a beach to ourselves, a gourmet meal, and a feast we would never forget. It was the honeymoon we would never have.

WHEN WE came back from our four-month backpacking trip, Rick and I stayed with Tanya in her apartment in downtown

Winnipeg. When Little Baba came to visit, she took one look at me and said, "You look like Farrah Fawcett!" All the hiking and swimming, not to mention a steady diet of rice and beans, had left us svelte but poor. We had used up our last bit of savings, so I applied for a Hudson's Bay card to buy food in the basement of their old building on the corner of Portage and Memorial. For his part, Rick used his connections to get a job in BC on a salmon boat.

In anticipation of our impending separation, we drank a bottle of mescal we brought back from Mexico and settled down for a day-long Scrabble tournament. We played our words with a vengeance. We arranged the letters like it was the end of the world and our scores would determine whether our souls would go to either heaven or hell. (I didn't believe in either.) We ate nacho chips, spread thickly with homemade guacamole, while the cats walked across the board, scattering our tiles.

After Rick left, I couldn't stop patting my pockets or checking if I had my keys. I couldn't shake the feeling that I had lost something. I missed the warmth of his muscly arms around me at night. I missed his broken front teeth from when he bit into a Costa Rican coconut shell. I spent my nights waiting for Rick's calls from pay phones on the dock where he stood in the wind and the rain to talk to me.

I planned to return to BC just as soon as I could earn enough money to put down a deposit for our own apartment in Victoria. I got a job as a bartender at the Oval Room in the Fort Garry Hotel, the same hotel where Big Baba had once worked. She used to entice me to eat the burnt toast on my plate by saying that was how customers ordered it at the Fort Garry. I never believed her and refused to take a bite.

I made great tips at the Oval Room. (I was heavy-handed with the Tabasco sauce when I stirred up spicy Caesars.) The room had high ornate ceilings and a grand piano in one corner. On weekends, a young woman would drape herself over it as she sang to a packed room, an old man in a tuxedo accompanying her. During the week, the room was filled with diehard gamblers who needed a respite from the hotel's Crystal Casino.

Every Monday morning at the start of my shift I vacuumed the carpets and furniture, zealously flipping up the cushions. My manager thought I was just thorough, but I was searching for the colourful plastic poker chips that fell out of loose pockets. At the end of my shift, I took the elevator to the seventh floor and used the chip money for the slot machines. My father gambled every day, but I left as soon as the money ran out.

In BC, Rick had made about thirty dollars after paying for his food and lodgings and travel expenses. He could have stayed in Winnipeg and lived off my tips. Desperate fish wife lesson #1: There is no relationship between work and money and no amount of pining will make it so.

Rick came back to Winnipeg, and we drove to Victoria in my Toyota Tercel. We rented an apartment, and I got a waitressing job. Rick left right away for urchin season. I learned how to strip-piece material and quilted it into leaping dolphins. I joined an adult ballet class and registered for a magazine writing course at Camosun College. During late-night dinners alone, I looked longingly at couples talking over plates of calamari and cheesy nachos.

One night after my shift at the Coachman Inn, I realized that I didn't want to go home to an empty apartment. Instead, I went to a nearby casino and played 21, doubling my tip money. I got to know people. I understood how a lonely person might be drawn to a room filled with warm bodies.

WE ARE all made of water: 60 percent of our bodies are comprised of it, and water collects in the heart, brain, and lungs.

Our unformed bodies float in the womb in a sac of water. On Winnipeg's slick sidewalks, my heavy waterproof boots had crunched in the snow. I never once thought of its liquid source just three provinces away in the Pacific. Yet it would seep into all aspects of my life, pour in, sweep me up, immerse me in a world defined by the salty sea.

My father smoked Player's Lights, and their logo was the profile of a sailor circled by a life buoy. I swore I would never marry anyone like my father, but perhaps I had associated my father, not with fire, but with what could extinguish it: the sea. While his nicotine-stained fingers fished for a stick in the crumpled pack at his dirty kitchen table, or on the dashboard above his overflowing ashtray, I cracked open a window even when it was thirty below. My father patted his pockets, hunting for that pack as he boarded Greyhounds driving away from me.

So perhaps it is no surprise that, like an old friend, I fell into the arms of a sailor.

My watery fate was also apparent in my penchant for Lena Horne's "Stormy Weather." In the '80s while people danced in the clubs to Madonna or Doctor & the Medics' "Spirit in the Sky," I went home to my pink futon, sipped red wine, and sang along to the Blues cassette in my ghetto blaster. I have always felt that I was from another era, a time when women in low-cut satin gowns slumped in corners of smokey night clubs with piano notes tinkling in the background, eternally mournful.

So many nights I would stare up at the shadowy ceiling holding my breath until I knew Rick was safely ashore. There was no stopping my tears.

HUEVOS RANCHEROS

This is a satisfying breakfast. Make up the sauce and pack the rest of the ingredients with you when you go camping. We have had success cooking the eggs in a pie iron between two corn tortillas over an open fire. A gourmet meal cooked over the campfire is always a big hit.

Serves 4

6 large ripe tomatoes	8 corn tortillas
2 large jalapeños	8 eggs, fried or basted
1 white onion, chopped	Queso fresco or sharp
Olive Oil	cheddar cheese (optional)
2 cloves of garlic, minced	For serving: fresh avocado
Salt to taste	slices or leftover rice

Broil the whole tomatoes and jalapeños over high heat. This will take approximately 15 minutes. Watch carefully so they don't burn. Flip them over to cook on the other side and then remove from the oven when their skins are browned and blistery. Cut off the stems. Blend the cooked tomatoes and jalapeños (skins and all) in a food processor until smooth.

In a skillet, fry the onions in a bit of oil until translucent (for about 10 minutes). Next, add the minced garlic and fry for a few more minutes. Stir in the pureed tomato/jalapeño sauce and cook over medium heat to boil off some of the liquid. Add salt to taste.

Meanwhile, in another skillet, fry the tortillas in a bit of olive oil over medium heat, but don't let them crisp. Place tortillas on a paper towel to soak up any grease. Place two tortillas in an ovenproof dish, top with fried eggs, and smother in the ranchero sauce. Grate or crumble cheese on top. Place pan in the oven and broil until cheese melts. Serve with fresh avocado slices or leftover rice.

TENDING TO LOVE

I WAS IN VICTORIA and Rick was in northern BC. One day he asked, "Why don't you come up and work for me, be my dive tender?"

"I wouldn't know what to do," I said.

"Anyone can do it. It's an easy job. I'll show you," Rick said. He was always trying to persuade me to come up north to work, to keep him company or to keep me from being lonesome, or a bit of both. We were to eat and sleep on Gil Bowman's liveaboard boat called *The Agonus*. Gil wanted me to join the crew to keep his wife, Sara, company. She was pregnant with their first child.

And so, in the summer of 1994, I travelled up to northern BC to Haida Gwaii (then known as the Queen Charlotte Islands), to work as Rick's dive tender. I had never worked on the ocean. My only skills on boats were gleaned from the two weeks a year I spent at Camp Stephens, canoeing with my best friend Carolyn Flower on the relatively gentle waters of Lake of the Woods. So, how had I found myself boarding the *Queen of the North* in Prince Rupert en route to the Haida community of Skidegate across fifty miles of the open Pacific Ocean?

The crossing would take six hours across the Hecate Strait, one of the most dangerous crossings in the world, thanks to extremely shallow waters and ferocious winter storms. On the boat, I obliviously followed Rick to the bar, where we joined other divers for beer and conversation to while away the hours. We sat under a framed photo of Queen Elizabeth and Prince Phillip in full regalia. Their smiles suggested they knew something I did not.

About two hours in, we hit open water. The captain had tried to stave off part of an incoming storm by taking another route through Beaver Passage, but when the ferry reached the open sea, the boat lurched without warning. Our whole table of drinks was levelled. We heard dishes in the kitchen crash to the floor. Everyone scattered in different directions. It was every man and woman for themselves. Rick and I fumbled our way to the hallway, looking for a safe place to wait out the storm. I didn't need the signs to remind me to hold onto handrails when the boat was pitching so badly. We were like pinballs ricocheting off walls.

A young boy of seven levitated for a moment before being thrown eight feet into a wall.

He got up dazed and limped away. Men were vomiting while Rick scrambled in the plastic tunnel in the children's play area. In John Vaillant's *The Golden Spruce*, the weather through Hecate Strait is described as "a malevolent weather factory." That day the waves were ten metres high. I was hurled along the hallway until I finally hunkered down behind a row of seats bolted to the floor. I braced myself for the long night ahead. I didn't sleep a wink but closed my eyes out of exhaustion.

The next morning, we disembarked and set foot on land, our shaky legs tottering down the gangway. Miraculously, I hadn't gotten seasick.

"It must be because you're from the Prairies," Rick said.

Oddly, I felt proud.

In 2006, the *Queen of the North* sank. The captain was off duty, asleep in his quarters when the boat hit a ledge of shallow rocks. There is a rumour that the navigator was having sex on the bridge with his ex at the time. In the court case, the navigator was convicted of negligence, and it seems pretty clear he was, at the very least, distracted by his ex-wife's presence. Two people died.

My job as Rick's dive tender included the important role of keeping an eye out for his bubbles (to make sure he was alive) while he was hunting for red sea urchins along the ocean floor. I was then to start the skiff's motor to go over to collect the full bag. My job also included hauling the urchins onboard with a hand-pulled winch. The streaming bag of live urchins was then dumped on the deck and had to be carefully placed in plastic stacking cages. I had to wear thick gloves to avoid getting urchin spines in my hands. My other tasks included pulling the anchor and helping Rick get in and out of his dive suit. If he had to pee, I unzipped the suit to help him urinate over the side of the boat. He wanted to prevent a wet spot in his dive underwear. I also lit his cigarette and placed it between his damp lips when he came up for a break.

While Rick was underwater for hours, I had time to think while I dutifully watched for his bubbles on the surface of the water. I enjoyed the peaceful slap, slap of the water against the metal hull of the small herring skiff. It had the name *Oak 18*. Rick didn't own the boat. He was leasing it.

I loved the clean air. Once when I pulled up the anchor, I noticed one perfect red urchin was wedged in between the metal bit shaped like a whale's tail, called the fluke. I grinned stupidly.

Rick popped his head up at that moment. "Why are you smiling?" he asked.

"I caught an urchin." I showed it to him proudly. I had Rick snap a photo of me holding the spiny globe with my oversized yellow mesh gloves.

The reality of my skills as a dive tender was that I was too weak to pull up the 250-pound bag of urchins over the gunnel of the boat. So, after a long day of diving, Rick would have to do most of the tending himself. He would haul himself up over the side of the boat to pull the bag of urchins up onto the deck. Together we would place them in the cages. Then Rick would start the motor and maneuver us safely back to the liveaboard boat.

Later we would eat dinner on the big boat where a pregnant Sara had made dinner for us, and then we would play Scrabble. I was always quite snobbish about playing Scrabble. Rick was quite a poor Scrabble player when we first met, but he was a quick study. Rick and I had a travel Scrabble board that we had taken with us tree planting or when we went camping in his orange vw van. It had little plastic grooves for the tiles, so they didn't scatter if you bumped them or if the wind shook your tiny home. Soon our games became extremely competitive. I was disdainful that Sara couldn't score high points. I don't think that I was the fun companion she had hoped for. As a vegetarian, I wouldn't eat her home-cooked meals of traditional meat and potatoes.

One day, Rick was diving in a little bay when the wind whipped up. Rick was working quite far away from the boat. His head popped out of the water, and he waved his gloved hands frantically. I knew he meant that I was to start the motor to pick him up. I had never been able to start the motor on my own; it was the kind where you had to pull a long cord. I was the kind of person who had never started a chainsaw or even a lawn mower—part of the drawbacks of being raised by a single mother and two babas. I secretly thought I would be able to start the motor if an emergency came up. I imagined I would find some deep inner strength like the Incredible Hulk, who uses his rage to split open his clothing with his huge muscles when someone is in need of rescuing.

The sky darkened and the waves got choppier. My stomach clenched in fear. Rick kept signally for me to drive over to him as the wind blew the little boat sideways. *Here is my chance to save the man I love,* I thought. I pulled and yanked at the engine cord but could not get the motor started. It sputtered a few times. But nothing.

Meanwhile, Rick was being sucked farther and farther away, and the boat was getting dangerously close to the rocks. I cried in frustration. I looked up to check on Rick and watched helplessly as he struggled against the rising waves and the current. I saw Rick take stock of the situation, put his head down, and begin swimming furiously toward the boat. He made it. He hauled himself overboard and started the motor before we hit the rocks. I sat in the corner of the boat, out of his way. I was wet and cold but mostly ashamed that I couldn't do my job. It turned out Rick was the Incredible Hulk and I was not.

Part way through this trip, Rick got a message from his family to come back to Fort McMurray at once. His mother, Louise, was dying. We travelled back to Prince Rupert on one of the fish packer boats in the region; it took two nights. When we reached the dock, the only spot to tie up the boat was next to a giant packer. To get to the dock, I had to climb up and over what look like an impenetrable mountain. I didn't think I could make it. The tiny ladder seemed an impossibly long way down to the wooden dock—maybe over fifteen feet, which to me seemed like a hundred feet. But I had no choice. I had to do it. With my thick grey socks in purple sandals, I gingerly placed each foot on the rungs. It was slow going, but, one by one, I got there.

We bought two tickets on the Greyhound bus back to Alberta. As we were driving along the highway from Calgary through Edmonton, our bus was the first on the scene of a bad accident. It looked like a small sport's car had hit a moose. The moose was splayed on the side of the road in a dark mass. The moose had taken off the top of the car like the top of a rolled back can of sardines. There was an enormous amount of blood and glass, and the driver was walking around holding his bloody head while the passenger was wedged, stuck in the crumpled wreck. (Later, I was reminded of this when Rick filleted his finger with an axle grinder and ran around the house showing our friend Esther a carpentry project while we waited for the ambulance.)

A man ran up the few steps of the bus and raised his arms. "Does anyone on the bus know first aid?

I hesitated. I had just taken a first aid class that spring, but I couldn't open my mouth. Once again, I was frozen in fear. In those few moments, three people jumped up ahead of me. I had sunk down deeper into my seat. To assuage my guilt, I offered up our sleeping bags to keep the two survivors warm. I was too afraid to speak up. The couple was bloody and desperate looking; they might even die. I was filled with shame that I didn't act.

Later, when we made it to Edmonton, the bus driver handed us the bloody sleeping bags in two plastic garbage bags and said, "Thank you. Do you want us to pay for the dry cleaning?"

We said no.

I stopped to visit my father in Edmonton and let Rick go on ahead to Fort McMurray to have special time with his family on his own. I imagined he wanted to have alone time with his mother and brother and sister. Perhaps I was afraid to be in close proximity to another dying mother and all the emotions it could unleash in me. After a couple of days, Rick called and asked me to come up because he needed me. And so, I did. His mom had such a strong faith in God that she refused any painkillers right to the end. She died soon afterward, in her own bed, with her family nearby.

It was about a week after Louise's funeral that I suspected I was pregnant. In fact, I always believed that I felt the moment of inception. There was a divine moment during our act of love-making where I honestly thought I felt the impact of a sperm reaching an egg. I know it seems crazy, but I have always believed that was how Hailey came to be, in a kind of cosmic balancing—Rick's mother left the universe and our baby entered.

Once my pregnancy was confirmed, I couldn't wait to tell my family, so I called long distance to tell Little Baba the news. She said, "Oh no!" like I was a teenaged pregnant mom on crack, instead of a healthy woman who had just put a down payment on what was to become a leaky condo.

Big Baba said, "Oh, tanks God!" in her Russian accent, which I thought ironic since I had never seen her enter a church in her whole life. I imagined her motioning for Avi, her fat loyal boyfriend with the watery eyes, to get the car warmed up so they could head straight to the baby department at the Polo Park Mall. I was twenty-eight years old. I knew in the old country I would have been considered an old maid. Once, years before, Big Baba caught me going out in what I thought was a cool men's vintage jacket. She saw me and yelled, "You look like the whore of the village!"

Prostitutes in Russia, I gathered, must have been poor women dressed in ratty clothes, desperate for work. I could tell by her voice that she was relieved that I was now embarking on a different path from the whore of the village—I was now tripping down the path to motherhood.

I was worried about giving birth, but I knew not to risk telling Big Baba about my mounting anxieties. She had stories that would cure any modern woman of what she would consider their ridiculous worries. I had a "husband" with a

job. A place to live. A clean hospital to drive to with real doc-
tors and nurses. Her birthing story involved going into labour
while working in the fields in northwestern Russia as armed
troops were advancing to take over their village. Although I
don't know the complete story, I imagine her bearing down in
a field of wheat taking sips of vodka while an inexperienced
friend whispered words of encouragement in her ear. Later,
delirious with fever after the birth of her son, she refused to
leave her bed as the town was being evacuated. Her neighbours decided to hoist her and her infant *with* the bed onto
the back of a horse-drawn wagon to rush them out of town. I
can almost hear the puffs of breath from the horse's nostrils
as they haul my baba and her crying newborn along the rutted dirt roads away from the soldiers and off to safety. Big
Baba's traumatic war stories are why any attempt to get an
understanding ear from her felt futile. I felt ashamed to ask
her if I should consider an epidural. I was hoping for a drug-
free natural birth, as close to birthing in a field as a modern
woman could get in a hospital.

My sister finally received the small pittance from our court
battle with Ronald. I used my portion of the money to pay
tuition for a resident care aide course at Camosun College
in Victoria. I was still clueless on how to find a job with my
recent degree in environmental studies, didn't know where
to look, who to ask. I had no connections, and home computers were barely a thing yet; there were no online job boards.
There were nursing homes on every corner in Victoria, so I
knew I was guaranteed a job after graduation. I was pregnant
while I took the course. When it was over, once again, I found
myself twiddling my thumbs in our new and soon-to-become
leaky condo, so Rick invited me to come up north to cook for
the crew.

WHAT TO EXPECT

I ADJUSTED MY BACKSIDE on the blue bucket we were using as a toilet at the stern of *The Buckaroo*. Across the water, an eagle dove and caught the twisting silver body of a fish, but it was difficult to appreciate the scenery. The plastic ridges dug into my flesh as I fanned my faded dress around my thighs so the divers wouldn't get an eyeful. My nose was running, and my feet were cold. There was no hot running water on board. It was the winter of 1995, and the rain was relentless. I was twenty-nine years old and in the third trimester of my pregnancy.

I had left Victoria to fly to the wilds of northern BC to share the excitement of our first child with Rick. We were living aboard a forty-foot houseboat he had bought with money he had inherited from his mother. Rick was working out of an inlet somewhere south of Prince Rupert, a slow five-hour boat ride from town to "the middle of nowhere" fishing grounds, spanning from the Juan de Fuca Strait to the Alaskan border.

TWO YEARS earlier, when we had first started dating, Rick and I had driven to Fort McMurray, where I met his mom, Louise. She knew I was a vegetarian and had made us spaghetti squash marinara. When his mother bowed her head in prayer, I looked up, unsure what to do, and saw Rick's sister Marianne make a funny face. I had to bite my lip to hold in my mirth.

Later, we played Scrabble around the dining room table, and when Louise wouldn't let me play the word "caveman," I was surprised but let it go. Rick later explained to me why: his mother didn't believe in the "story" of evolution. His parents had met at bible college, and his mother was deeply religious. To be polite, Rick and I slept in separate rooms.

After Louise died, Rick and I didn't talk openly about our grief but learning about the pregnancy so soon after Rick's mom's death was a bittersweet moment for both of us. In addition to the houseboat, the inheritance had also allowed us to purchase a small condominium in Victoria—a tiny two bedroom with a small deck off the third floor where we could peer into the townhouses across from us. During the day I would walk, stomach first, down the streets of Victoria as strangers asked to touch my protruding belly. I was desperate to share my pregnancy with Rick, so when he called on his satellite phone, I cried and gratefully agreed to join him and the four other divers who lived and worked on the boat.

I booked a flight as soon as I got off the phone, and, a few days later, Rick met me at the airport in Prince Rupert. Before we headed out to sea, we stayed at the Moby Dick Inn. When I stepped out of the shower in our motel's bathroom, I got a full view of my naked body in the mirror.

At home, I could only see myself from the neck up. I was not prepared for the shock. "I'm a troll," I said. "A giant troll!"

Rick said he still found me attractive—so I made him prove it. "I won't hurt the baby, will I?" he asked.

"It says on page 221 of *What to Expect When You're Expecting* that this is perfectly safe, and, in fact, we should do it more often as the due date gets closer."

It is odd to want to perform an act of reproduction when nature has already taken care of that. I couldn't get enough of making love—hormones were running rampant through my body. This, too, was explained in detail in the book. *What to Expect When You're Expecting* was my constant companion. I had read it on the flight and would read it constantly over the next several months. I flipped through it in bed, read it on the toilet, and out loud at breakfast. Each chapter contained practical and scientific information, but I attributed a kind of divine wisdom to it. I found answers to questions I didn't know to ask. This was the '90s, before Google became a verb, a world of screeching dial-up internet connections and landlines. The only way to get information was from books, friends, or family. I was terrified about our impending parenthood; I wished I had a mother to ask for advice.

When Rick bought *The Buckaroo*, he converted the bathroom into a bunk to cram in two more divers. He charged a crew of four divers a nominal fee to live on the boat to help pay for fuel. Normally, no matter the weather, the blue bathroom bucket was forbidden inside the boat, but I had to pee numerous times each night, so Rick made an exception. He couldn't have the mother of his first-born fall overboard in the dark of night. We slept on the converted dining table. Every night I wiped crumbs from the tabletop and transformed it into a double bed. In the dark, under a mass of sleeping bags, I whispered bits of newfound magic to the back of Rick's neck: "Our baby now has eyelashes."

Each day it got harder to get up off the blue bucket. I had to grab the slippery metal railing to get my balance before heaving the contents overboard with a splash. I had imagined my days on the boat would involve listening to CBC while reading in the sun, that I would cook elaborate meals for Rick and the other divers who would, in turn, compliment my culinary skills. Of course, nothing ever happens the way you expect.

Rick left each morning on the *Oak 18*. He picked red urchins with a simple hand-held metal rake, custom fit for his arm. The gap between the rake's two fork-like tines was set at four inches, an adult urchin's circumference, so divers would harvest adults and leave the undersized. Rick would clutch a large mesh bag with one arm while swimming along the seabed, sometimes eight hours a day. A full bag would be about four feet long and hold over two hundred pounds of urchins.

In the evenings, I hounded Rick to describe his underwater world. He revealed snippets from his workday: swimming scallops, their shells flapping comically like false teeth, or the pesky fish that followed behind him, snacking on broken urchins. He told me the fish swam into his net and he had to stop to untangle them. Once a sea lion playfully dragged him along the bottom by his black rubber fin. He told me how baby urchins, the size of a button, were flung away in the current when he harvested the larger ones hiding beneath them.

While the men splashed around in the surf all day, I walked up and down the three steps to the wheelhouse. For exercise, I would flick on the radio and break a sweat by stair-stepping in my thick grey socks and purple sandals. When I got tired of the Anne Murray songs that were played on the Prince Rupert stations, I pulled out my yellow Sony Walkman to listen to the Ramones' "Beat on the Brat." Perhaps this was not the best song for a mom-to-be to listen to.

In addition to my pregnancy manual, I had brought the *Moosewood Cookbook,* filled with vegetarian recipes. This was my favourite cookbook, and I referred to its splattered pages on a weekly basis. The first night on board, I proudly plunked down a steaming pot of curried chickpeas and rice. Rick scooped up a heaping bowlful and made an appreciative "Mmm," but the other ravenous divers just looked at the pot and said, "Ah, where is the meat?" They found a pack of hot dogs, boiled them up, and ate them plain.

The next day, as I was opening a tin of tomatoes, Rick, who rarely raises his voice to me said, "No! Stop. It's bad luck to open a can upside down on a boat," but it was too late. I had already opened the can, label side down. Men on boats take their superstitions seriously.

A FEW weeks later, the weather shifted. Walking across the galley felt like being in a fun house. Rick forced me to go to the back of the boat so I wouldn't witness the raging waves that were battering the wheelhouse windows. Born and raised in Winnipeg, I wasn't prepared for a violent storm at sea. Hands slick with sweat, I grasped the metal railings to go below deck and teetered over to the table. Rocking on the choppy waters of the Pacific Ocean, I was conscious of the fact that the only thing protecting my unborn baby was a bit of amniotic fluid and the thin, stretched outer skin of my enormous belly.

The weather report predicted a week of storms, so Rick decided it was time for a break and piloted the boat back to Prince Rupert. When we arrived, Rick begged me to get on a plane with him and go back to Victoria. I stubbornly refused because I had read in *What to Expect...* that flying is not advisable in your last trimester.

Rick thought I was crazy, but he let me go. He knew I was adamant to keep my baby safe from premature birth. The trip was over thirty hours with many rest stops at seedy-looking depots. I subsisted on egg salad sandwiches on soggy whole wheat.

Rick flew back to Victoria solo, but he couldn't stay with me for long in Victoria; he needed to get back up north. He promised to make it back in time for the birth in May. A couple of weeks before I was due, he travelled from Haida Gwaii, over fifty miles of open sea, on a listing fish-packing boat called *The Sea Rake*. It was very stormy, and he was seasick, but he wanted to make it home in time for the birth of our first child.

In our delivery room at the Victoria General Hospital, I stood in the shower in a long, arduous fog of contractions too far apart to be taken seriously while Rick flipped through pages of *What to Expect*... Around midnight, a nurse popped her head in the humid room to ask how things were going.

"I'm pretty tired," he said.

"I meant your *wife*," she said.

WHEN THE delivery nurse announced it was a girl, I blurted out, "I'm sorry!" Perhaps I shouldn't have read *The Joy Luck Club* during pregnancy. I had presumed Rick wanted a boy, but it was probably for the best. I can't imagine a life with mini-Ricks, daredevils jumping off the roof of a garage. Oh, the accidents! Or as soon as they could, marching off to sea.

A few hours later, when Rick first held our baby's tiny, swaddled form, he did so awkwardly, like he was afraid she would break. Rick went home for the night, and I sent her to the nursery so I could get some rest, but minutes later I hobbled down the corridor in bare feet because I couldn't bear to be parted from her. With weak arms, I pushed the enormous plastic trolley back to my room, where she slept next to my bed. I checked a hundred times to see if she was still breathing.

We had a long discussion on what to call her and chose Hailey, because Haley's comet was racing through the skies. Rick had wanted to call her Ocean, but I said what if she isn't an ocean and doesn't like the sea? Years later, I see she could have been an "Ocean," was very much an ocean. She took to the water like a fish.

The first week home, I thought I really needed some breast pads for the milk that I didn't know would harden my breasts and leak constantly, creating dark wet spots on my clothing, so I took Hailey out with me to the mall. The woman behind the counter of the bakery peered at Hailey's little scrunched face and admonished me, "Too small to take out in public; no good for the little one."

I knew she was probably right. Oddly, the power went out in the mall, all the lights blinked out, and I had to hike down the stalled escalator with Hailey wrapped inexpertly in her little flannel blanket. Rick hadn't wanted to shop for breast pads, so we had separated. When we found each other, my legs were shaking with fatigue, and Hailey had screwed up her face in a way that I knew was leading up to yowling unless I stuffed a nipple in her mouth.

We hurried home because I felt weak, which surprised me. I had imagined that I might be one of those women who could work in the field hours after giving birth. I was wrong.

CRADLING HAILEY in the sling a few months later, I felt stronger. As I strode through the bustling streets of Victoria on a clear summer morning, I imagined that I was an adult sea urchin using protective spines to shelter my young. I quickened my pace—I wanted to hunt down a copy of *What to Expect the First Year.*

On one of my last doctor visits, I had asked my doctor if it would be okay to travel with an infant to attend a wedding, and Dr. Walton said, "Sure! Best time to travel, when they're young."

I trusted him, so we strapped Hailey into her car seat in the vw van, imagining it would be like one of our earlier cross-country road trips, before children. The first night we pulled into a campground and Rick picked up Chinese food.

I was to nurse Hailey and put her to sleep and meet him around the campfire. Two hours later, Rick poked his head into the van.

"Nope," I said. Hailey's next crying jag ended at 2 AM. This was to be the norm through the rest of the trip. I must have been too tired to have read the chapter in *What to Expect the First Year* about colic spells and how to stop them. It was difficult to pace the length of the van with a cricked neck.

The next night we stayed in a motel, but Rick slept in the van so he could get enough sleep to drive the next day. We cursed our doctor and started parenthood like many other before us, with no clue about what to do. I also had been reading too much about how to be environmentally conscious and had sewed cloth diapers for the trip. It didn't occur to me that a baby would blow through twenty diapers in an instant, so I had to buy an extra-large pack of disposables at our first stop. I didn't understand that babies often nursed at all hours. I thought they might nurse at breakfast, lunch, and dinner, taking a total of twenty minutes tops for all three meals. I didn't know newborns might like to nurse for long periods of time, and, when out in new places, they might get distracted by new sights and sounds, and could get too riled to eat. Rick drank too much at the bachelor party, oddly held the night before the wedding. At the wedding, Hailey was wailing, and I fumbled to get my leaking breast out to feed her while leaning into the damp bathroom counter. I was mad and tired and couldn't wait to get home.

It was the start of our life together as new parents. I was living through what so many new mothers throughout history had already experienced—my partner's world and mine were drifting off in new directions.

CAESAR SALAD WITH HOMEMADE CROUTONS AND FRIED CAPERS

Homemade croutons will make this salad a standout at potlucks.

Serves 4

Dressing

A big squirt of Dijon mustard

2–3 medium-sized garlic cloves

1 Tbsp Worcestershire sauce

2–3 fillets of canned anchovies or 1 Tbsp anchovy paste

Big chunk of blue cheese

1 coddled egg yolk (Coddled means to dip the uncracked egg in boiling water 30 seconds before using. Crack the egg to then use in the recipe.)

½ lemon, juiced

1 tsp balsamic or red wine vinegar

1 tsp ground black pepper

¼ cup freshly grated Parmesan cheese

⅓ cup olive oil

Croutons

Dry bread (preferably a French baguette), cut into ½-inch squares

Melted butter

Olive oil

Salt and pepper

Dried oregano

Chopped, fresh parsley

1 garlic clove, chopped

Dash of grated Parmesan cheese (optional)

Fried Capers & Assembling Salad

1 jar of pickled capers

Flour

Olive oil

1 large head romaine lettuce

For the dressing, Blend all dressing ingredients except for the olive oil in a food processor or blender. Slowly drizzle ⅓ cup olive oil into the blender or food processor and mix until thickened.

For the croutons, preheat oven to 325°F. Add chopped bread to a bowl. Add melted butter, olive oil, s & p, chopped garlic, dried oregano, and chopped fresh parsley to cover the bread pieces. A dash of Parmesan cheese is also nice.

Bake croutons in the oven on a flat cookie sheet until golden brown and toasted.

To make the capers, drain the liquid from a jar of pickled capers. Coat them with flour. Fast fry the capers in a large skillet with a bit of oil until golden.

To assemble the salad, add lettuce to a serving bowl. Add the dressing and toss until lettuce leaves are coated. Sprinkle fried capers and croutons on top of your salad.

WHAT CAN YOU DO WITH A DRUNKEN SAILOR?

IT WAS MIDNIGHT when I stood over Hailey's squirming body, bleary-eyed, steadying myself with the fake wooden ledge of the change table. As a cocktail waitress, I carried full trays above my head using my forearm as a protective shield through crowds of drunken revelers. I pulled up steaming bags of urchins as a dive tender. I won fifty dollars in a karaoke contest singing Nancy Sinatra's "These Boots Are Made for Walkin'" as a lip-syncer. Yet how did any of this qualify me to care for someone so small, so breakable? I preferred to have my nose in a novel. Now I couldn't sit down to read for more than a minute before being interrupted by Hailey's fussing for my leaky breasts.

In our tiny apartment, her tinier lips clamped to my nipple. All I could see were hand-sewn flannel diapers, triple padded in pastel colours with baby ducks on them, that had to be rinsed and thrown in the washer. They had taken hours to sew on my Singer sewing machine in the dining nook. I honestly thought, even after rereading *What to Expect When You're Expecting*, that babies ate three meals a day. I believed they would sleep a full night, after a fairly short-lived, colicky stage. I didn't know the stage could last for months.

I was on my own in a city where I hardly knew anyone, worrying about keeping a baby alive. Most nights I sat by myself stress eating batches of chocolate chip cookies, washed down with a jug of milk. I wore an ugly grey plaid shirt unbuttoned, breasts flapping, to let Hailey nurse and for some peace and quiet. During the day, I hung a sheet across the balcony railing so no one below could see in.

During pregnancy I thought I had a free pass to eat whatever caught my fancy. I made banana bread from Rick's mother's set of *Women's Day* magazines, made with lard instead of butter. *Lard!* I ate the whole cake myself. Rick took me to the Cheesecake Factory a few days before the due date, and I could hardly fit in the booth.

WHEN HAILEY was only a few months old, she got a high fever and a stuffy nose. I had to suction out the bubbling snot with a plastic bulb that looked like a miniature turkey baster. Hailey fought it furiously, turning her little head incredibly fast for a baby. I admired her strong spirit. In that moment, I thought about my own mother's single parenting days, how lucky she was to have Sonia to ask for advice when she found me sleepwalking, nimble as a fox, nipping through the carpeted hallway in bare feet to make a midnight escape into the snowdrifts.

Unable to translate Fahrenheit to Celsius, I was worried about Hailey's fever. I bundled her up and waited anxiously for hours in the hospital's emergency room. I stood helpless in the hallway as a nurse with rough hands forced a bottle of fluids past Hailey's pursed lips. Her little face was purple from squirming and crying all night. We got home at 7 AM after her fever broke.

The next morning, as Hailey lay asleep in a messy heap on the bedcovers, I called Little Baba, just to hear her voice. She always seemed prickly when I called these days, so I didn't mention the rough night. I missed her piercing blue eyes, a surprise of colour from her wrinkled face, the rest of her, all bones and sharp points.

Little Baba told me she had nearly died in childbirth because of her narrow hips. "After giving birth to your father, I couldn't have any more children."

We had spent many a long evening playing Old Maid at her Formica table, next to the comforting roar of her Frigidaire, my grandpa out of sight in the living room reading the *Winnipeg Free Press*. I imagine her as a young woman pacing the small patch of kitchen linoleum in the dark of a Winnipeg winter, a colicky infant over her shoulder. My grandfather is out drinking and carousing and just as she gets my father to sleep, he stumbles in and wakes the baby. She dares to complain. He gets mad and hits her. She comforts a crying baby with a dislocated shoulder. Once, in an act of defiance, Little Baba burned Grandpa's favourite neck scarf on the stove element.

Maybe if I needed advice, my best bet was a women's group at the local community centre. A nurse was scheduled to give informative talks to new mothers once a week. It had taken me months to feel Hailey was more than a warm weight in my arms, but I couldn't tell Baba that.

I eventually rolled up my milk-stained sleeves and joined a mother's walking group. The first meeting was at Beacon Hill Park. I stood outside the petting zoo for over an hour. It finally dawned on me that I had gotten the date wrong. I maneuvered the baby stroller into a large bathroom stall of the public restrooms and wept over Hailey's little flannelled body. I was desperate to talk to grownups, other mothers.

I didn't give up. I figured out the next meeting, got the time right. I knew I had to ferret out moms with infants wherever I could. I picked up *Island Parent* magazine and put an ad in the classifieds for swapping child care.

Rick's phone calls, once welcome, now became an intrusion. He seemed to call when I was just walking in the door with a crying baby over my shoulder and heavy plastic bags of groceries cutting off the blood to my fingers. I had completed an impossible task: strapped our child into a car seat, found parking, picked up avocados or apples in the aisles without waking her, paid, loaded the car, put her little squirming body back into the car seat, and he had the nerve to ask, "How are you?"

"Can't talk now. Just walked in the door. Hailey's crying." Food has rolled out of the bags and across the kitchen floor that needs washing.

Or, after one of Hailey's nightly crying jags, I would stumble back to bed exhausted only to be shocked out of sleep by the harsh ring of the telephone.

"Margot, I love you sooo much."

"Are you crazy, calling me now? I just got Hailey back to sleep. It took me almost two hours."

"But I just had to tell you how much I love you." His voice was slurring with drink.

"Don't call me when you are like this," I said, hanging up. He would call me right back.

I began unplugging the phone before I went to bed. *What can you do with a drunken sailor, early in the morning?*

I GOT a job as a nurse's aide, which involved shift work at the nursing home, Mount St. Mary Hospital. At home, I changed baby diapers; at work, I changed the soiled diapers of ninety-year-olds. Strangely, I loved it. One resident held a doll in her arms morning to night, convinced it was her baby. *Is this where mothers end up?* I wondered, lying in a hospital bed, wearing soiled white gloves, holding a fake baby until their dying breath? I wanted to be the lady who silently laughed to herself, eating pudding with her fingers, ignoring the spoon on the tray. I hoped if I cared for Hailey properly, she might not stuff me in a care home.

I had found child care help by following a woman named Maura through the underground parking lot of our condominium complex, and boldly knocking on her door. She lived in the apartment building across the way, and she said she was available to babysit. I could call her at 6 AM and say, "I've got a 7 AM shift, so I'm bringing her over now," and she would say in her thick Irish accent, "Okay, I'll be ready." Maura lived alone. Her son had died of HIV. "Not because he was gay, mind you, but because of a blood transfusion," Maura said.

When I picked up Hailey she wanted to sit on the balcony and smoke and talk, but I was impatient to get home. She didn't seem to know anyone in Victoria either. She had raised her son, working as a seamstress.

She knitted Rick an intricate sweater and sewed Hailey fancy little dresses. I was inclined to put Hailey in clothes from Value Village, considering she crawled around in the dirt, drooled, and just wanted to be comfortable. I bought clothes that worked for a boy or a girl, in case we had another baby, trying to find ways to save money.

I picked up Hailey after my 3 to 11 PM shift at the seniors' home, put her in the baby carriage, and pushed her home, hoping for an hour to myself before I crashed.

When Rick came home, I trailed him into the bathroom to talk to him through the steam of the shower, desperate to talk to a grown-up. I told him things only parents found fascinating. If I left for some time on my own, Hailey would weep, face burrowed into his shoulder, until I returned two hours later. His whole T-shirt would be dark with her tears. It was like when men came back from the war, who frightened their own flesh and blood.

ONE DAY Rick strapped Hailey into the car seat, closed the car door, and realized the keys were in the locked truck. He panicked, rushed back to our apartment, and shouldered in the door to get the spare key. When he returned, she didn't even look distressed. She hadn't noticed he wasn't in the driver's seat. He had been on his way to my work, so I could nurse her on my lunch break, but she was too distracted to nurse in new surroundings.

At home I cried as I pumped; I didn't want to leave her for eight hours, six days on, two days off.

Why have children you can only see when you are worn out, worn thin, and not at your best?

WHEN HAILEY got older, Rick had another adoring fan. When he walked through the door, in a full beard, dropping his stinking dive bag at his feet, she would crawl up his body, wind her little arms around his neck, and squeal, "Daddy!"

I would go grocery shopping—a free woman at last. When Rick was home in his off season, June to mid-August, he was in charge of Hailey, so I could pick up as many shifts at the nursing home as I wanted.

Rick made homemade perogies, Caesar salad, a whole turkey, and a fancy chocolate cake in the shape of a whale with Smarties and icing for Hailey's birthday party. We hauled the whole feast to Beacon Hill Park and asked Rick's brother Adrian and his sister Marianne to join us. We also invited Rick's Polish diver friend and his family, friends from Mount St. Mary Hospital—in short, anyone remotely close to us.

ONE DAY I walked in the door, back aching from turning old people in their hospital beds to avoid bedsores, and hung up my car keys to find Rick baking a blackberry pie with Hailey, shirtless and covered in flour, her face stained purple. I was shocked. I thought of my father—our weekends together, going out for Chinese food, chicken balls smothered in syrupy sweet and sour sauce or to fast food joints for greasy onion rings. I didn't realize a father would take his child to pick berries along the Galloping Goose Trail and come home to bake pie with her little unpractised hands. I fell in love all over again and happily swept the floor.

I realized then that I knew exactly what to do with a drunken sailor, any time of day.

DEEP DISH BLACKBERRY PIE WITH SHORTBREAD CRUST

Making heavy pie crusts is hereditary. Big Baba's cookies and pies all had the same tough dough, but I never complained. Chubby little girls like me were happy any time someone handed them a treat. No one complains if you set out a homemade pie in front of them, with a thick, buttery shortbread crust—or not.

Makes one 9-inch pie

Pie Crust

1 cup unsalted butter, cut into 1-inch cubes

½ cup unbleached cake and pastry flour

1 Tbsp granulated sugar

½ tsp cinnamon (optional)

¾ tsp salt

1 egg, beaten

2 Tbsp ice water + more if needed

Filling

6 cups of blackberries
for a deep-dish pie (if
using frozen blackber-
ries, defrost and let
liquid drain off before
using and up the corn-
starch amount)

½ cup white sugar
½ lemon, zested, optional
(gives it a real lemon
zing)
⅛–¼ cup cornstarch

To make the dough, in a food processor, blend the butter, flour, sugar, cinnamon, and salt until a course meal forms.

Beat the egg with the 2 Tbsp cold water and add the liquid to the food processor. Blend until a wet ball forms. (Add a little more water, if dough is not coming together.) Divide the dough in half and cover with waxed paper or preferably bees wax wrap! Place in the refrigerator until you are ready to assemble the pie.

Preheat oven to 350°F.

To make the filling, in a mixing bowl, gently mix together blackberries, sugar, lemon zest and ⅛ cup cornstarch. (If your berries are very juicy, add more cornstarch.)

Roll out each disc of cold dough in between waxed paper so they don't stick to the rolling pin. Carefully place one disc into a deep dish pie pan. Pour in the filling. Place second piece of dough on top and crimp the edges with the tines of a fork. Make attractive slits in the top if you desire to allow steam to escape.

Bake for 1 hour. Cover the edges of the pie so they don't burn, either with foil or a handy silicone pie crust shield. Allow the pie to cool completely before cutting it.

CHRISTMAS AT
THE VISTA DEL MAR

ON DECEMBER 1, 1999, less than two weeks after our second daughter Chloe was born, we packed up the contents of our small condo in Victoria and moved to a three-bedroom house on Brydie Road on Gabriola Island. We had taken a road trip to Gabriola to look around the fifteen-kilometre island with a real estate agent a few months earlier. I peered into someone's big picture window to see adults standing around with brimming plates of food, laughing, while in the yard balloons waved from the fence post and children chased each other around a huge apple tree.

This scene sold me on the island, not the deer grazing in the ditch, not the corridor of trees locals called the Tunnel. I longed for rooms filled with people, for parties, for a connection to community.

RICK DROPPED us off at our new home but he didn't have time to stay and unpack; it was his busy season for diving, and he had to leave immediately.

"I'll be fine," I said. "Don't worry about us." My words came out braver than I felt. I couldn't work, so we *needed* him to pay the bills. It was a strange and unsettling new feeling to rely on someone else to provide for me. It was a hard adjustment as I was used to supporting myself.

Chloe was ten days old, a babe in a house in the woods, rented for 750 dollars a month. It had two stories with a fenced yard and a wood-burning fireplace. I unpacked just enough cutlery, bowls and one lonely pot for cooking. I was too dazed to tackle the rest, when I realized I was about to raise a bored four-year-old and an infant on an island, without a vehicle. There was no public transit to take us to the grocery store or to the pharmacy.

The first three weeks I walked around in a dream state, exhausted from Chloe's crying, so by the time Rick called and proposed spending Christmas at a hotel in Campbell River, I was too dazed to argue. Besides, I felt sorry for Hailey. Green urchins were fetching a good price, so Rick wanted to keep working throughout Christmas. He would pick us up in his leased Ford, and we would celebrate at the Vista del Mar Motel—Vista del Mar means ocean view, but we could only see the ocean past the busy Island Highway.

Campbell River was dreary in the wintertime when tourists had abandoned it and left it to loggers and salmon fishermen who were used to the wilds of northern Vancouver Island. It is rugged country, an ideal filming location for movies such as *Seven Years in Tibet* and *The Scarlet Letter.* The Elk Falls Mill was the biggest employer in town until it shut down in 2009. The last time I was here, before the kids, I'd worn my *Pardon me, though bleeding piece of earth* T-shirt, showing a clear-cut forest. Rick nervously pointed out this wasn't the ideal fashion for a logging town. Now Campbell River promotes itself as the "Salmon Capital of the World" to draw in tourists.

I didn't think tourists would be staying where we were. Our room had a tiny kitchenette with white brick walls and windows lined with heavy plastic curtains. I kept them closed, trying not to feel guilty when I parked Hailey in front of the TV. I could hardly keep my eyes open with a mewling baby permanently attached to one of my breasts. To save money, I made my trusty vat of curried chickpeas with rice.

I CLOSED my eyes while I stirred, trying not to sleep, just resting for a brief, blissful moment or two, swaying with a fussing baby over my shoulder. I hoped the movement would calm her as I served Hailey, interrupting her fourth straight hour of *Caillou*. I walked the length of the cramped motel room, adjusting the long men's grey plaid flannel shirt, tucking and untucking my leaking breasts while bobbing and cooing to get Chloe to sleep.

I ate the curried chickpeas and then nursed Chloe again, resulting in her experiencing severe stomach pains and more tears. To offer some reprieve to Hailey, we walked across the highway to make a game of skipping stones in the ocean. When Rick got home, we went out for dinner, but, after diving all day, he too had only so much energy.

The next day I made plans to visit a local photographer to take professional baby photos of Chloe. Every time I look at the pictures now, I re-experience the extreme fatigue of that time and fixate on the dark imprint of her forehead birthmark, made by the forceps that would grow darker when she screamed. Our pain is captured forever in sepia.

While we were in Campbell River, Rick remembers taking Hailey out for a swim at the local pool and going to a movie to get her away from the dank motel room that smelled of leaking breast milk and curried chickpeas. "It was a nice bonding time for us," he said. "Why do you always remember the bad parts?"

When I thought of Rick at sea, I never imagined him to be lonely, though he must have missed us, and it was only in these passing comments that I learned otherwise.

In the evenings, I pulled out materials for crafts on the miniature kitchen table and made handmade Christmas cards to keep from going stir crazy. I cut out our faces from the family photos we had taken and put them on handmade sketches of reindeer or Mr. and Mrs. Claus. This was before Photoshop, but we were able to make photocopies of our cards, luckily for all who received them.

The old couple who ran the motel felt bad for us—a family stuck in a motel for the holidays, so they forced a fake Christmas tree on us. I was too polite to turn down their kindness, despite the cramped quarters, so, I cleared away the glitter glue, and we started decorating a tree with red and gold balls and crumpled garlands that looked and smelled like they were from the 1970s.

In the end the market for urchins dropped, as it always does, and we returned home for Christmas Day. I hardly remember it; I was so exhausted after nights of fitful sleeps and a wet mouth clamped to my nipple.

As the new year and the start of the twenty-first century approached, Y2K was on everyone's mind. The end of the world was nigh. So, we bought a one-hundred-dollar bottle of champagne and tried to keep our eyes open until midnight. We were unsuccessful, and so the bubbly remained corked.

The world didn't end, and there were plenty of islanders around in 2000 to invite their new neighbours over for a turkey dinner. At first it didn't look good—some guests got stumbling drunk and one of the children was in bed with a fever, but our daughters played well together, recipes were swapped, and I had a sense that this was the beginning of something.

EASY CURRIED CHICKPEAS WITH RICE

Serves 4

½ cup of plain unsweet-
ened yogurt, divided
2 Tbsp curry paste
(I like Patak's Mild
Curry Paste)
Olive oil
1 onion, chopped

2 celery stalks, chopped
2 large carrots, chopped
1 can (540-mL) chickpeas
rinsed well.
2 sweet red apples, sliced
Sunflower seeds (optional)
For serving: brown rice

In a bowl, combine ½ cup of plain yogurt with curry paste and set aside.

Boil up a pot of brown rice. I always make enough to feed an army. I suggest cooking 2½ cups of dry rice to have enough rice for leftovers. While you are waiting for the rice to cook, fry up the veggies in a bit of olive oil until softened. Rinse the chickpeas well and stir them in the pan with the cooked veggies to heat thoroughly. Mix in the curry/yogurt sauce. Take off heat and stir into the brown rice, top with sweet apple slices, and sprinkle with sunflower seeds so that everyone knows you are a hippy.

STEPPING STONES

RICK TOOK our Ford SUV to Campbell River to return to work, as this was normally his busy season so I was left to amuse a four-year-old without the help of friends or family while I attended to the needs of a cranky baby. Not having transportation was not sustainable, so eventually we got an old black BMW with leather seats, and I drove around the island exploring beaches.

One of the first things I did was drive to the Community Hall to enroll Hailey in preschool. Being a city girl, I mistakenly believed there would be an administration office with forms to fill out and classes to choose from. When I pulled up to an empty parking lot and a locked building, I was shocked. I stood outside in the cold, next to the wide trunk of a maple tree, wondering how I would meet other moms. I cried as I drove the winding road back home—Beacon Hill Park all over again.

I eventually found the preschool phone number and enrolled Hailey only to discover that it was a "parent participation" preschool, so I had to help clean the bathrooms and volunteer on specified days, bringing Chloe after a special exemption was made for me to do so. I would strap her onto my back, chatting with moms on the playground while the kids found garter snake nests or played on the swings.

I invited the whole preschool class to the house for Hailey's birthday in May that year.

My new friend Kathy dressed up in a long blonde wig and brought a homemade tickle trunk filled with dress-up clothes. I made a piñata and a chocolate cake, which parents ate wandering through my living room. Now children were running around *our* fenced yard, and balloons streamed from *our* fence post.

Kathy came over sometimes to read Hailey bedtime stories while I dealt with her crying sister. Hailey had sprayed perfume in her own eyes to register her discontent. I yelled at Hailey, "Why would you do this?" But I knew why; she had to do something to get her mother's attention.

To use my brain as well as my body, and to stay sane, I started a book club. This club became so important to us that one woman showed up a day after returning from the hospital after birth to her fifth child. During the summer, I sat under the shade of a spreading big leaf maple at Twin Beaches sharing parenting tips with the other moms while our babies crawled in our laps and put sand in their mouths. The older kids would lift up rocks to find tiny crabs or chase each other half-naked through the warm, shallow waters. I had found a community and it was incomparable.

I longed for Rick but had to make do with his disembodied voice on the other end of the phone from the Moby Dick Inn in Prince Rupert. (I called it the Moby Rick.) I knew the phone number by heart. Rick had certain rooms he favoured: "The TV in this one is better," or "I like the bed in this one." He was always coming home with the plastic key chains, the return address stamped in gold on the back. I would dutifully slip them back into the mailbox but eventually gave up; there were just too many rattling around in the bottom of his dive bag.

When he was away, we talked on the phone about nothing and everything. We talked as he walked to the bathroom to pee, while he opened the door to the pizza delivery man. I told him what I made for dinner, about my great find at the recycle depot, about Hailey's teacher who said she was talking too much in class. He told me about a baby orca that followed their fleet and blew a spray of fishy water at him.

One Friday I sat in the darkened living room, opened up a bottle of wine, and called him for a little bit more than conversation.

"What are you wearing?"

"I'm naked," I lied. It was chilly in the house, and I wrapped the ratty blue bathrobe the girls had bought me for Christmas more tightly around me; on my feet I wore Rick's thick but holey dive socks, keeping my toes warm.

"You're naked. Really?"

"No. Not really," I admitted.

IN THE winter, Rick worked in Prince Rupert, and there was storm after storm. He was stuck in a motel for over a week, hoping for a break in the weather to get back to work.

One afternoon, after I dropped the girls off at school, and went home with plans to chop kindling he called, bored.

"Lucky you," I said. "Why don't you see if there's a place to go swimming, like a rec centre or something?"

"Yeah maybe. Do you think, um . . ."

"What?"

"What are you wearing?"

I laughed, not wanting to be a poor sport. I closed the curtains, as if someone could see me blushing through the woods. The closest neighbour was miles away. I went into the bedroom, closed the door.

"I am in that black lacy thing you like."

"I do like that one . . ."

"I'm... wait. Hold on, there's a call on the other line... Hello? Oh, hi, Sarah. No, I don't think it's working, but let me ask Rick. He's on the other line... Rick, sorry, it's the neighbour. She needs to borrow our chainsaw. Did you get it fixed?"

"No, I don't think so. Remember I drove over it?"

"I remember. Just a sec... Hi, Sarah? No, we don't. It's broken, too. Sorry! Okay, bye!... Where was I?"

Later, in the grocery lineup at Village Food Market, I dreamily stared at the smoked ham and smiled, remembering the rest of the call.

Over the years, I got over my inhibitions and found the right words. Sometimes after I hung up, the empty silence of the house was almost too much to bear.

Sometimes, though, I resented his calls, when I was just getting off the ferry, or unloading bags into the house. Why wasn't he here to help carry the heavy cooler laden with Superstore's free frozen turkey?

There were times I felt like the only cure for my ennui was a bottle of red wine and Billie Holiday's honey-dipped voice in the background.

TWO YEARS later, we moved out of the house on Brydie when the owners decided to sell it.

We found another rental on Martin Road. I cleaned the house while Rick was away. The girls were bored with their toys packed away. Chloe grasped the edge of the wallpaper that was peeling and ripped it clean off in a strip. I had splattered pink paint on the cheap curtains in the dining room, where I had been painting things to sell at the farmers' market. We didn't get our damage deposit back.

We had to come up with another damage deposit for the new house and pay for someone to haul away the garbage. There was no end to the expenses, and living on the edge was taking its toll.

The new house was a sprawling '70s place on the south end of the island, up a long, winding gravel driveway. It was perched on top of a rocky hill, overlooking the government dock. The landlord, Nick, lived in a smaller house right next door. It was $800 a month, and we could bring our cat, Cosmos (we called her Kitty), so we struck a deal.

Hailey was now in Grade 2 at Gabriola Elementary School. In order to save money on gas, I would walk her to the bus stop, down our long winding gravel driveway, down the road that curved along the ocean, a fifteen minute walk away. I had to leave by 7 AM to get her to the bus stop, pushing Chloe along in her stroller. Our house was far away from Gabriola Elementary, which meant Hailey was gone until 4 PM, when the school bus finally finished its loop around the island to arrive near a spot called Gossip Corner and our stop. Gossip Corner is at the south end of the island, where pioneers used to wait for their postal deliveries. Now there is only a faded sign that remains.

On the way home after dropping Hailey off at the bus stop, Chloe and I would stop at the dock to lie on our stomachs and watch for sea creatures—large shadows darting under the dock that both intrigued and frightened us. After school, we liked to fish off the dock and were surprised when we actually caught a fish. I had to pull the hook out of its mouth to cries of "Don't hurt it, Mommy!" Hailey wept as I threw it back in the ocean.

We stopped fishing after that.

AT HOME I pushed Chloe on a little wooden rope swing that hung from a tree, painted with red ladybugs. I was always painting dragonflies, ladybugs, salmon, mermaids, and whales. After the girls were in bed, I painted light switch covers with purple Van Gogh irises on them to sell at the farmers' market every Saturday morning.

The landlord surprised me by digging right under our front picture window and applying ant spray around our doorway without consent. He had a big old dog named Baby that chewed on the whale vertebra that Rick had brought home from Haida Gwaii. There was brown shag carpeting in the bathroom we replaced with cheap linoleum, and though the house had a lovely view, I was too busy experimenting with natural soap and skin care recipes to notice, holding melt-and-pour soapmaking classes for ten in my kitchen. I had put an ad in the *Gabriola Sounder*: MAKE SOAP BY THE SEA, $50 PER PERSON.

At night, I took online writing classes from the library, learning how to write children's books, which I illustrated with pen and ink. During the day, I taught children's art classes at the Women's Institute Hall. I took any job that allowed me to bring Chloe along; she was always strapped to my back or perched on my hip. Hailey was happy when Kathy's daughters, Anya and Mara, dropped by to spend the day hunting tiny lizards, hiding in rocky crevices. The short walk to Drumbeg Beach was a good spot for catching the critters. Or they made blackberry smoothies from our endless supply of berries stocked in our deep freeze in plastic Ziploc bags.

Our neighbours on the other side often shot off guns, and as there was nothing but forest between us, I couldn't get a clear view. I imagined a gang of drunk hillbillies in stained yellow undershirts, spitting chewing tobacco and taking pot shots at seals, so I told the girls never to go near their fence. Little did I know they were real estate agents who entered the annual Potato Cannon Contest on July 1.

Maybe I shouldn't have been so quick to judge, considering I discovered a bloated tick attached to Hailey's neck. I called the nurse hotline and they said to use tweezers to pull it out properly to avoid the risk of getting Lyme disease.

I couldn't find any tweezers in my jumbled-up drawers, so the nurse recommended getting it removed at the hospital. This would mean packing up, waiting in a ferry lineup, and the cost of a hotel room in town if we were still at the hospital after 11 PM, which was when the ferries stopped for the night. Rick was on his way home from Prince Rupert, and I had to pick him up at the ferry anyway, so we piled into the car and sang along off key and with false bravado to "I'll Be Home for Christmas" while I imagined a bloated tick sucking Hailey's infected blood.

Rick walked through the passenger gate with a full beard and his large dive bag full of dirty clothes from a month-long trip. I walked up to him, dragging Hailey behind me, handed him the neighbour's pliers, and said, "Pull it out properly, and we won't need to go back to Nanaimo."

He took the pliers, held back Hailey's curly hair, and neatly pulled the fat tick out, head and all. Our knight in shining armor saved the day again. He was our reluctant "king of the world." He even muttered that phrase in his sleep.

Rick could only take ten days off and had to turn around and go back to work up north. This hardly seemed like enough family time to me. As soon as he left, I called my friend Kathy to complain. "Why can't he find work closer to home!" She recommended we try couples therapy. Soon after, we attended counselling. The therapist suggested Rick work toward a job that would keep him closer to home. Rick enrolled in a boat-building program at the Silva Bay Shipyard. I was certain things were changing for the better.

GROWING UP in Winnipeg, when everyone was still alive and healthy, before my mother's cancer and before the long hospital visits to my grandfather's bedside, where he lay shaking and demented with Parkinson's disease, we would all meet in Big Baba's dining room for a family feast. We gathered for many Jewish holidays, and my zayda would sit at the head of the table and recite prayers in a language that I didn't understand. When I was six, I would crawl along the carpet underneath the table to steal the shoes right off the feet of the grown-ups. I made them pay a paper dollar each for the return of their shoes. I remember the leather pumps, still warm from their toes. My uncles Victor and Harvey would get boisterous after drinking bottles of beer and pretend they were Cossacks, kicking their feet out in front of them.

I will never forget my first taste of eye-watering horserad-ish or the saltiness of gefilte fish, small, unappetizing, pale ground balls. I can still hear my baba's voice: "Eat! Eat!" It was her mantra. Even though I was overweight, and usually full, I still allowed her to pile my plate with homemade per-ogies, slick with butter and sour cream. Seated at the long dining room table, surrounded by my family, laughing and bickering, I felt safe and warm, the sound of snow hitting the windowpane sideways, a common sound in Winnipeg in the wintertime.

Big Baba loved to cook. I can only picture her in her kitchen, always in motion, wiping down counters, always cooking—the cool fabric of her dress swirling against her legs as she moved. Later in life, she had a television moved into the kitchen so she could watch her soap operas as she worked. "Oy, such a bad guy!" she would say to the characters as she cooked and watched, cooked and talked.

As a young girl, I would stand on a chair in the kitchen and stare at her thumb. It was cut off at the knuckle and reminded me of the twisted end of a pickle. I would watch her cut out the dough for perogies with the rim of a glass, her strong hands white with flour, and I would badger her. "Does it hurt? How did it happen?"

But her answers never satisfied me. "Oy, dare-tee" she would say. "I fell down when I was a baby." I thought this pet name for me meant something special in Russian, but when I asked, she told me in her accent, "It means you run around and get dirty, so I call you dare-tee."

I was disappointed.

She loved to garden. Sometimes I would walk the half hour to her house from ours, trailing my hands through the fragrant dill plants towering in the backyards of the modest houses in her neighbourhood. Big Baba grew a line of tomato plants against the sunny side of her house, tied to stakes with pale-coloured nylons. I would lie on the puffy lounge chair cushions in her backyard, painting my nails, and watching her, topless, as she ironed on hot days. "Oysht, it's hot!" she would say as she flapped her enormous breasts up and down to air them out.

One year she returned from a trip to Florida with a suit-case full of seashells. She spread them throughout her garden between brightly coloured plastic flowers that she took in every winter to wash, storing them between old towels until the spring. If it was raining, I spent all day in the basement rummaging in old trunks, reeking of mothballs. In the dark of the basement, I playacted with neighbourhood kids, my neck wrapped in real fur stoles that my zayda had sewn in the back room of his furrier shop.

Big Baba had enjoyed many trips to Hawaii. She always came back loaded with gifts for her family, suitcases that she first filled with frozen chicken wings that she had breaded and fried and placed in big plastic bags to take to their Hono-lulu apartment. We hated everything she brought back for us—enormous rings, shell necklaces, gaudy shirts—but she looked so joyful as she unzipped her huge suitcase, that we could only smile and thank her. Later, we'd throw them into a dark corner of our closets. I still have a blue zippered bag of cheap costume jewelry in the bottom of a cardboard box—small sea turtles inlaid with fake rainbow shells, clunky rings. I can't bear to throw them out.

Her life was filled with hard work. My mind conjures a scene of her in the countryside in Russia, tied to a millstone, walking around and around in circles, grinding wheat—no money for a mule, just a little girl in a kerchief with bare, muddy feet wearing a path in the dirt.

I am grateful for my Grade 7 family tree in the back of a book titled, *Stepping Stones to Seven*. On the last page, there is an image of a tree beside a stream with white stones along the bottom. In neat, blue handwriting I placed my name first, to the left of the tree trunk. The rest of the family I fanned out with small arrows to the left.

My baba's real name is Neura Litvinov, not the anglicized version of Anna, born in 1917, the year the Russian Revolution began. People were hungry and desperate; millions died in the civil war that followed.

Next, I wrote her mother's name, Nadia Simionovna, then the grandmother who raised her, Tanya Trigubova. That's all—the men don't exist. Lost in war, lost with no trace, like stones thrown into the middle of a deep lake.

Big Baba loved caring for her family. I used to sit next to her on the front steps of her townhouse in my nightie, naked feet on warm concrete, carefully maintaining the edge of my ice cream cone with my tongue. She told me that one day that when her husband died and we were grown with families of our own, she would kill herself. She went on to explain that we would be busy taking care of our own families, so she wouldn't be needed anymore. I only thought about this conversation years later when she took too many sleeping pills—her first attempt to end her life. This was after the deaths of her daughter-in-law, her grandson, her husband, and then my mother. She also outlived her new boyfriend. Was it too much loss? The tiny pebbles of it starting to roll when she was a small child in Russia, given to her grandmother when she was only two, to be raised, because her mother's new husband didn't want her.

When I received a phone call about Big Baba's suicide attempt, I flew out to see her. We sat in the visitor's lounge in the hospital, her eyes staring at the television screen too low to hear, and she said without a smile, "You came?"

A few months later she was found hanging in her bathroom from the metal curtain rod.

I didn't go to her funeral. I was worried about the cost of another plane ticket, but I thought of her often when I taught my daughters to make homemade perogies or the delicious meat-filled dumplings we called kreplach, served boiled with butter and plain mustard. I felt a flutter of pain when I looked at my oldest daughter, who loved to wear sparkly jewelry and bright flowery skirts—she reminds me so much of her. My youngest daughter's graduation dress was embossed with brilliant, beaded seashells like those dress-up clothes I played with in Big Baba's cool basement on those long winter days in Winnipeg. I am saving old clothes in my own closet for future grandchildren. When they come to visit me, I will have them twist off the ripe tomatoes from the vines in my garden, where we will sit together, listening to music, talking and laughing, swatting at mosquitoes, as I serve the tomatoes still hot and thickly sliced, with salt.

RUSSIAN *PELMENI*

Like many things in our family, recipes have been mixed up and borrowed from other world cuisines. Our family refers to these meat-filled dumplings as *kreplach*. *Kreplach* are traditional Jewish dumplings, which are normally stuffed with ground chicken or beef. Big Baba called them *pelmeni*. She filled them with a mixture of ground beef and pork. I am referring to them as *pelmeni* because the way Big Baba made them, with the ends pinched together like tortellini, most resemble traditional *pelmeni*.

Makes about 50 pelmeni

Dough

1 large egg, beaten
⅔ cup of milk
¾ cup water

4 cups unbleached white
    flour (or use OO pizza and
    pasta flour), plus more
    flour if needed
1 tsp salt

Filling

2 Tbsp oil or butter
1 white onion, sliced
1–3 large cloves of
    garlic, minced

Approximately 2 lbs finely
    ground meat, such as
    beef, pork, or veal
Salt and pepper

Cooking the *pelmeni*

Small amount of oil

For serving: butter and Dijon
    or yellow mustard

To make the dough, stir together the beaten egg, milk, and water. Using the dough hook of a stand mixer, slowly add in the flour until it is smooth and not too sticky. Add more flour if needed. (You can also make the dough in your bread machine on the dough setting.) Cover dough with plastic wrap or a damp towel and let rest for at least an hour before using.

To make the filling, heat the butter or oil in a large skillet over medium heat. Sauté onion and garlic until softened. Remove from heat and add to a medium-size bowl. Let cool. Add ground meat to the bowl and mix well. You can use any combination of ground meat. My local deli offers a combination of ground beef, pork, and veal which is a nice combination. Big Baba used a mixture of ground beef and ground pork. A nice vegetarian filling alternative is to fry up some minced garlic in butter and stir in finely chopped mushrooms. Add salt and pepper to taste.

Big Baba used a rolling pin to roll out the dough and the rim of a water glass to cut out the rounds. I have discovered that running sections of the dough through the pasta maker is a wonderful way to create a thin, consistent dough. If using a pasta roller, start on the largest setting (1) and then run your well-floured dough through the roller, carefully holding the thinning dough with both hands. Change the pasta roller setting, in increments, to 2, then 3, and finally 4. If the dough is too thin, it can tear. Keep dough covered with a damp towel while you roll out portions of it. Instead of a water glass, I use a round 3-inch cookie cutter to cut out the rounds of dough.

After dough has been rolled out and cut into rounds, spoon about a tablespoon of the meat (or vegetarian) filling into the middle of each circle of dough. Fold each round of dough over into a half moon shape and pinch the edges closed. The last step is to bring the two ends together so that the shape looks like a round tortellini. Set the filled dumplings out on a floured, flat baking sheet, and freeze the ones you don't eat for dinner. They can then be placed into a covered container and put back in the freezer for a quick and easy meal.

Bring a pot of water to a boil. Add salt and a small amount of oil. Drop the *pelmeni* into the water. Do not overcrowd. Boil for 10–13 minutes. Use an instant-read thermometer to make sure the meat reaches 170°F. Strain in a colander. Toss cooked *pelmeni* with butter and serve with Dijon or plain yellow mustard.

I NEVER PROMISED
YOU A ROSE GARDEN

WHEN A FRIEND told me of a cabin coming up for rent on the island, we swooped in. The house was perched on a cliff with long, winding wooden steps down to the sea. It was at the end of a short gravel road that ended at a public access trail to the ocean. The school bus stop was also only a two-minute walk down the lane without any traffic.

Across the street from the property was an empty, beautiful two-storey house with two red brick chimneys and a gabled roof. It had rose bushes fifteen feet high growing along the garden fence and trailing up the trees that dotted its trimmed lawn. I noted enviously that they could afford to have landscapers water and prune. A caterpillar's nest on a blackened branch had been torched—how mysterious. Only the birds and deer enjoyed their craggy moss-covered apple trees. I imagined the house had insulated windows and a certified fireplace, enough room for a family of four, *and* their dog and cat. It probably had at least two bathrooms and a proper washer and dryer, not just a cold-water washing machine in a shed across the lawn.

The point felt private, and our pie-shaped property had stairs down to the beach. Even the outhouse that had an ocean view. We affixed a long, laminated scroll of a cross-word puzzle from the *New York Times* that we'd inherited from Rick's mother in Fort McMurray, but we never once used the outhouse or tried to do the crossword.

The cabin had an orange metal fireplace that was striking but emitted no heat at all. There was an old oil furnace that cost seven hundred dollars to partially fill, and this only kept us warm for two months. This cramped, dark furnace room was initially Chloe's bedroom, though it barely fit her single bed. (It reminded me of Harry Potter's tiny room underneath the stairs of the Dursleys' house). There was a huge add-on behind the kitchen, which had many windows and its own door to the backyard, so I moved the girls in there together, and Rick and I took the smaller bedroom that Hailey had been sleeping in.

In the heat of a fight, I once yelled at Chloe, "Go to your room!" I shut her in her bedroom behind the kitchen and began to make dinner, furiously rattling pots and pans.

A moment later I heard the outside door open and the sound of her little marching feet on the front deck. She had walked around the house in her bare feet, opened up the front door, and said, "No! You go to your room!" and slammed the door. I heard her march back around the house and enter her room again. She had to get the last word in.

There was no dryer, so I had to drape our wet jeans on a wobbly wooden clothing rack in front of the fireplace. On Thanksgiving, to not feel that we were without family, I took the girls to visit Rick's brother in New Westminster on the mainland. We were sitting around their fancy dining table with another couple, when I realized with horror that we reeked like a smokey campfire.

In the summer, I hung our clothes on a clothesline, and the wind from the ocean dried everything quickly, but I always had mounds of cleaning rags to dry. I had started cleaning houses for twelve dollars an hour. Cleaning was the best paid job for women on the island, so I tried to fit a job in between dropping Chloe off at Kindergarten at 9 AM and picking her up at 11:45.

I grew weary of not having a dryer, so we picked one up off the side of the road. The only place to plug it in was in the kitchen, so we set it next to the kitchen table. We had to run the vent out of the window, adding to the draftiness of the place. It was so cold that during the winter, we had a secondhand electric heater, but it kept blowing a fuse and killing the lights.

We were still cold, so most nights from September to April, I would fill up our bathtub with hot sudsy water, the girls standing in the doorway naked and ready to join me. It was only a standard-sized bathtub, but, somehow, we managed to wedge our bodies in to warm up.

Rick began his classes at the wooden boat-building school. The BC government paid for his tools and tuition, and he got a small amount of money from unemployment insurance every month. I was hoping it would persuade him to make the leap from diver to woodworker. I imagined him coming home from work every night, kissing me on the cheek as I stirred up a pot of chili, and tousling with the girls. This was not to be.

We were industrious, at home and at work. One day, I came home from cleaning houses to find Rick in the kitchen, cooking up half a side of beef that had defrosted when "someone" had left the small front-loading deep freezer open. He made multiple roasts and hamburgers and then refroze it all.

During a break from boat-building school, Rick returned to diving to earn money. If Rick couldn't make it home for a holiday, it would throw me into a depression. I had enough energy to make dinner and serve it up, but happy banter was beyond me. The only sound around the dinner table was chewing. I would stare blankly ahead while the girls chattered away to each other. The cat mewled at my feet, setting my teeth on edge. Kitty was always hungry and ate until she puked—just another thing for me to clean up. I wanted the girls to go to bed so I could sit on the couch and drink myself to sleep, watching old movies.

To make matters worse, we got an anxious street dog I named Stella (after my favourite beer) who would tear the house apart while I was away cleaning. I'd come home to garbage strewn around the kitchen floor, the pillows from the couch ripped to shreds. I felt tricked into getting her. My mantra to Rick was "You can have a dog when you are home full-time."

Rick said, "Well, here I am at boat school, home full time now."

I couldn't argue the fact and he won. I came to detest the 2 AM wake-up calls when she barked to be let out. I worried she might soil the carpets. She bolted out the door, almost knocking me down in pursuit of deer, while I stood naked and shivering on the doorstep, calling "Stella!" (Yes, I named her Stella, for that very reason.)

I cooked dinner every evening while listening to the dog's high-pitched frenzied barking down at the beach. Stella didn't like the water, so she only dipped her paws in, plunging her snout into the cold water to pluck out a rock to chew on. I knew the girl's location by the racket.

Hailey and Chloe spent whole days collecting starfish and minnows, storing them in plastic containers, until they let them go. Hailey was such a pro and used her bare hands. I have a photo that Rick snapped of Kitty and me on the front page of the *Gabriola Sounder*. As the tide rose, the cat grew more and more anxious until she had to make the plunge and swim to shore.

The girls played for hours collecting sea life while I made soap and dinner, soap and dinner. Once they even discovered a dead octopus.

Later, after the girls were in bed, when Rick wasn't home, I painted Van Gogh irises on tiny light-switch plates and wooden Ikea mirrors and garden crates. I ate enormous slabs of chocolate cheesecake washed down with milk while I watched sad movies. I collaged *National Geographic* photos I collected at what islanders called the depot or GIRO (Gabriola Island Recycling Depot)—a popular outing for us every Wednesday and Saturday. On our weekly visits, I would hand Hailey and Chloe a handful of change and allow them to choose a plastic toy from the bin. It was the one place where I rarely said no; it felt good.

THE CABIN had an enormous arbutus tree that stood picturesquely in front of the deck. With this ever-changing view, we hardly cared that we didn't have cable. I planned to take a photo of it daily, like the character in the movie *Smoke* (played by Harvey Keitel), who takes photos of his store every day at 8 AM. Each day, the view past that tree was wildly different. I never did snap photos daily, and I always regretted it. I watched as the sunrise and sunset danced on the orange bark and the way it took on a magical sheen in the rain. Once a year, the thick trunk was covered in snow. I had always wanted to paint that tree but I never did.

We held the wedding ceremony for Rick's sister Marianne and her husband on this property. They chose it for its shimmering water view. Unfortunately, I hadn't yet learned the proper way to turn compost, and it stank to high heaven. It was a wet, reeking mess. The entire wedding party was upwind. People were too polite to say anything, including a friend who was playing the viola in a string quartet next to the outhouse. Chloe was the flower girl in a borrowed black and white gown, and I wore a dress that cost ten dollars from Value Village.

IN ADDITION to house cleaning, making soap and painting driftwood that I sold at the Gabriola Farmers' Market, I also scored a job organizing the Gabriola Youth Softball League four times a week. Rick was a volunteer coach and the girls got free lessons. I took the gear home and cleaned it in our bathtub when I found mouse droppings in the helmets. I bleached everything and set it out in the sun to dry. At the end of the season, I received a $1,000 cheque I cashed to buy soap supplies.

At this time, I was often working seven days a week, fitting in batches of soap while the girls played, bringing them to work with me if they were sick. I cooked every meal from scratch.

I scrubbed bathrooms and mopped wooden floors between kayak camp or gymnastics camp. The girls ignored their list of chores—walk the dog, do the dishes, clean your room—instead lounging in their pajamas watching TV, with the dishes crusted over in the kitchen. I would walk in after work and blow my top.

"If you two had done your chores, we could be heading to the beach right now!"

It was me that was craving the beach. Later, when we got to Sandwell to swim, I sat on the warm sand and read Sebastian Barry's *The Secret Scripture* or *The Scarlet Letter* for my book club.

Rick said I should get a better job with my education, but on this island, I felt it wasn't possible. I could work at Village Food Market for minimum wage or commute to Nanaimo, but I would need to pay for a babysitter and be gone for twelve hours a day.

Besides, he was one to make suggestions when he seemed to work hard *not* to make money. For example, Rick was a skilled self-taught jeweller and stone carver. When an artist named John Ogilvy got engaged, he asked Rick to cast a gold band for his wife's wedding ring. The night he went to deliver it, I made a special minestrone soup with homemade stinging nettle pesto and a loaf of sunflower seed bread.

When Rick walked through the door, the girls ran to him in excitement. He was carrying a very large square painting, about three-feet-by-three-feet.

He said, "Look what I got!"

I said, "How much money did he give you for the ring?"

"Nothing. He gave me this painting instead."

"You're joking, right?"

"No, this is what he gave me."

It was a painting of a road with a cut block on it, in dark greens and browns.

THAT CHRISTMAS was a meagre one. Chloe, who didn't know any better, was happy with the Zellers embroidered pink flower jeans, rubber boots, and a game of Monopoly from Santa. I recycled last year's mechanical dog (paid for the pricey battery) and told little Chloe it was Christmas magic. She believed me. Hailey, who was in on the Santa secret, told me that she was pleasantly surprised with her gifts after I had warned her to brace herself in case she was disappointed.

It was at this little cabin that I hosted Hailey's tenth birthday party sleepover in May and told a gaggle of girls the story of "The Yellow Eyes" around the campfire. I cut out tiny rubber yellow balls that fit over my eyes and penned in eye holes with a black Sharpie. I slowly turned around and popped the yellow orbs over my eyes and ended the story with a flourish. I can still hear the girls' high-pitched screams.

One year I brought in a clown for Chloe's birthday; another year we had a spa party. We played pin the lips on Justin Bieber and made fancy cupcakes with Day-Glo icing. We played Survivor and Pass the Present.

We had crab feasts on the deck when Rick brought home a Puget Sound king crab, its bright orange-and-red plate of horny armour surrounding enormous claws. We ate crab cakes, drinking wine and laughing, moving the kitchen table outdoors, shuffling dining chairs to find patches of warm sunlight. Sometimes the kids acted out whole plays and reprimanded us if we tried to talk, so we had to talk in whispers, giggling like we were the children and they were the stern adults. When the girls got earaches on the weekends from the wind, I had to pour warm olive oil in their ears and use a blow dryer until I could get to the pharmacy on Monday morning. I learned to keep a special bottle of ear drops and antibiotics for emergencies.

Every summer we had to leave for two weeks when the owners came to enjoy their cabin.

They slept in our bed and looked after our cat, but not very well. She ran away because they stopped feeding her, but she came back when we returned. We couldn't afford to take time off from work, so we put up three small tents in the Gabriola campground, one for the girls, one for us, and one for my FilterQueen vacuum and cleaning supplies. Stella was a nuisance; she barked whenever she heard a sound. We made the best of it. Rick was working at the Nanaimo Shipyard that summer and could be home by 5 PM for a swim. One night we had a giant crab feast sitting at the wooden picnic table, enjoying each other's company.

Sometimes we house-sat for our friend Marin, whose bedroom had a large tree through the floor and an enormous bed and TV. We watched *Eat Drink Man Woman*, drank Lucky beer, and made love in her apple orchard among ancient, gnarled trees. In the fall, Marin held huge apple press parties and we all went home with giant freezer bags full of sweet brown apple juice.

KALE, BEET & BACON SALAD

In Winnipeg, we made my favourite salad with simple ingredients: fresh picked tomatoes, green onions, and finely chopped iceberg lettuce, dressed with oil, white vinegar, salt, and black pepper. I loved the sour tartness of the white vinegar mixed in with the liquid of the tomatoes so much that I drank the dressing left at the bottom of my bowl. Since moving to BC, I now include kale in many meals because it is so hardy and grows almost year-round. Even on the rare snow days on Gabriola Island, I can still find stalks poking out from our raised garden beds. If you don't have kale in your garden, baby kale from the supermarket works fine. This salad is a meal in itself, with a lovely tart tang from the beets cooked in apple cider vinegar and a simple vinaigrette coating the kale leaves. If you use, regular kale leaves, massage the shredded leaves with the juice from half a lemon to soften.

Serves 4

Dressing

½ cup olive oil
½ cup apple cider vinegar
3 Tbsp Dijon mustard

2 Tbsp maple syrup
½ lemon, juiced
1 tsp garlic salt

Salad

3 large beets, cut into
small cubes

¼ cup cider vinegar

½ lb (225-g) package
of bacon

1 large red or white
onion, sliced

1 package of baby kale
(this is also nice

with a combination
of spinach and kale)
or 1 bunch of regular
kale, shredded

Black olives, sliced

1 sweet apple, thinly sliced

1 avocado, cut into
small cubes

¼ cup feta cheese

For the dressing, whisk together, olive oil, ½ cup apple cider vinegar and Dijon mustard. Whisk in the maple syrup and lemon juice. (If using only kale leaves, massage a little extra lemon juice into the leaves to soften.) Add garlic salt.

Add the cubed beets to a saucepan with enough water to cover and ¼ cup of cider vinegar. Bring to a boil and cook until al dente. Remove from heat. Fry the bacon in a large skillet until browned, and set aside to drain on paper towels. Pour off most of the grease and leave a little bit in the skillet to fry the onion slices. Cook onions slow and low until they turn golden brown and sweet. Set aside. Cut or crumble up the bacon into small pieces.

Dress the kale leaves with the vinaigrette, making sure to coat all the leaves. Serve greens in an enormous pottery bowl. Top each serving with a healthy portion of beets, bacon, olives, apple, and avocado. Crumble the feta cheese on top.

10

THE MIDDLE
OF NOWHERE

THE WINTERS were too cold to live in a drafty cabin by the sea, so after a few years we heard through the grapevine about a log cabin across the island on Seymour Road on five acres. Rick drove up to look at it in his rumbling truck, his hair a wild mass of orange, his broken front teeth, his holey clothes, his paint-splattered shoes. The owners said yes on the spot. There is something about Rick's freckled face that people trust.

It was seven hundred and fifty dollars per month for a two-bedroom, one-bathroom log home. It was surrounded by trees in every direction—one leading to an open field with a large oak tree and a tire swing.

Hidden in the back was a dilapidated tree house. The children could spend countless hours outside, hunting for fairies, picking wildflowers, or making daisy chains. The house also had a huge fenced garden with the branches of apple and plum trees grazing the garden bed, which was overrun with cornflowers and raspberry canes. In the yard, kids could camp out during birthday parties or guests could stay in a tent like a spare room.

We would learn that the previous owner rebuilt the cabin after moving it from somewhere in the Okanagan. His ex-wife, named Boo Champion, planted the garden. I would get her mail for years, magazines from Greenpeace and Birder's World and UNICEF. I had always wondered what she looked like and eventually met her in a pottery class in Nanaimo. She looked upset when she learned I had lived in her beloved home. Each tree and flower, like the California lilac against the shed, had been planted strategically with an artist's eye.

There was no ocean view, but, once we moved in, we could sit on our couch and see out a large curtainless window, overlooking flowering rhododendrons and ferns, and see deer with their felted horns munching on the tips. Sitting in the familiar dip of that couch, I could see a Luna moth, tender muted green, the dark night behind it. I sank back into the soft cushions and sighed with wonder.

Cleaning houses and the extra income from Starfish Soap Company afforded me the freedom to be there for the kids after school every day. I made thousands of bars of soap to sell to tourists and a growing list of island customers. I brought the girls to the market on Saturdays and Sundays. Chloe would colour or play in the grass and Hailey would get stuck in the branches of the trees she was compelled to climb.

I made soap in the kitchen and dried the bars all over the house, so it stank of patchouli and peppermint. It clung to our clothes; scents wafted from our hair. When Rick worked on his off-season at the Nanaimo shipyards, the men catcalled him because he smelled so "pretty." Chloe walked down the lane with wet hair and a towel, and I could smell her patchouli from a half mile away. Like Pig-Pen from *Peanuts*, we had a cloud wafting around us, only ours was of exotic clary sage, fresh lemongrass, and sharp rose geranium.

At the market, I tried to remember each customer's favourite soap, and what they were allergic to, lavender or rosemary. Marcelle the potter liked fir needle soap and was allergic to tea tree oil. People hunted me down, just for my pink Himalayan salt bars or gardener's hand soap with scrubby orange peel. Some wanted foot moisturizers; some bought my perfumed tins for their children to take to summer camp so they would not be lonesome for home.

I picked nettles in the marshy area at Whalebone Beach to make into pesto for slathering on top of homemade pizza. I brought two Ziploc bags, a pair of scissors, and a rubber glove. I cut off the top leaves with the scissors, so they fell in the bag underneath. Besides making pesto, I also used the leaves for making my popular geranium and lavender nettle shampoo bars.

I put the nettles in a colander and rinsed off any bugs, then picked out the big stems using a pair of metal tongs. I boiled distilled water and poured it over a pitcher of the nettles and left them to cool. Then I pureed the nettles with a hand-held blender. This green soup became the lye water portion of the soap. I stirred it into the heated oils, then poured the thick batch into a large plastic bin, greased well with olive oil and a paper towel. After a day or so, I cut it into thick chunky bars, and set it out to dry for four to six weeks. These are Rick's favourite bars because he can wash his body and wild mass of hair at the same time.

WILD-CRAFTED STINGING NETTLE PESTO

Pesto doesn't have to be made with basil. You can substitute boiled stinging nettle leaves for the basil. There are two species of stinging nettles found in Canada. They can be sourced in wet forested areas or marshy areas or along streams and ditches. Pick your stinging nettles in early spring when they are fresh and fairly bug free. Use a pair of scissors to snip the top few rings of leaves, and hold a Ziploc bag underneath to catch them.

Note: Use gloves and a clean pair of scissors to remove the stems from the leaves. Discard the stems as they can be tough and fibrous. Rinse the nettles in a colander and use tongs to place the itchy leaves in boiling water. Boil for 3 minutes. (Boiling takes away its sting.) Squeeze out the water and use the nettles as you would basil leaves in a traditional pesto. You can also make pesto out of just about anything green in your garden. Use the curly tops of garlic (called scapes) or beef up a basil pesto with fresh kale or leftover spinach leaves.

4 cups freshly picked
    nettles
¼ cup olive oil
¼ cup grated Parmesan
    cheese

2 or 3 cloves of garlic
¼ cup of walnuts
Fresh ground black pepper
Salt to taste

Makes 1 cup

To process fresh nettles: Using clean kitchen gloves, sort through the nettles and pick out any bugs, sticks, etc. Rinse nettles in the colander. Place nettles in boiling water (put them in using tongs) for 3 minutes. Drain in colander, then squeeze out excess water with your hands.

Place your freshly boiled and squeezed nettle leaves in a food processor with the rest of the ingredients. Blend until the garlic and walnuts are pureed, and mixture becomes a smooth paste. Add more oil if needed to create a thin consistency. I find the Parmesan cheese adds enough of a salty kick, but taste and feel free to add more salt if needed.

Slather nettle pesto onto a homemade whole wheat pizza crust or toss in hot pasta. Pour into little ice cube trays to freeze. The high oil content makes these pop out easily. Store in a Ziploc for later use.

ALMOST EVERY evening I cleared away the dinner dishes, wiped down the kitchen counters so I could stir up batches of soap. Later, I sat at the kitchen table and labelled each bar by hand or made up gift baskets. The table was always crowded with my soap-making paraphernalia, so we often ate meals in the living room with our plates balanced on our knees. After the busy Christmas season, I'd make pot sticker dough from scratch and tortillas with masa harina flour for a taco dinner. They were less tasty than the ones in Mexico we ate fresh from the screenless door of the tortilla factory, but flavourful all the same. I also made broccoli and filo pastry, nettle tea with peppermint, homemade flax bread, and almost every morning a batch of waffles with leftover butternut squash thrown into the batter. The garden gave us raspberries, apples, plums, rhubarb, and Swiss chard. Every night I was at the bottom of what islanders called Brickyard Hill, picking berries to lay on cookie sheets and put in the deep freeze.

However, I was a terrible gardener. I overwatered or under-watered. Our tomatoes split from too much water. I couldn't bear to pull anything up, even small flowering weeds. I let parsley grow in between rocks and the uneven rows of lettuce. The raspberries went wild, and I let them; cornflowers self-seeded; and the rose bush wound itself around the fence. Despite my lack of a green thumb, I somehow grew spinach and Swiss chard into the early winter, even after rare light snowfalls. Sometimes if a horse went by, I would run behind it to collect its droppings for our garden.

After all the soap making, especially during my busy season at Christmas, I grew tired of so much time in the kitchen and when making dinner I started to relying on frozen perogies fried up with a few onions and bits of chard I found in the garden, with a handful of frozen peas. Hailey got upset at all this pedestrian fare and taught herself to make a full roast chicken dinner every Sunday from scratch. For a twelve year old she already had a knack for cooking up complicated meals. She tried a new recipe every week. I remember her stuffed spinach Mediterranean chicken and teriyaki chicken.

It was here we raised two batches of fifty chickens with Cathy and Roger Perry, who lived up on Hess, a few minutes drive down a winding road, fairly close, by country standards. They had two boys who attended Gabriola Elementary with Chloe and Hailey (in different grades) and Cathy was in my book club, the Bookeroos. Rick and Roger commuted on the same ferry when Rick worked at the Nanaimo Shipyard. Sometimes they cycled down the same winding forest trail, emerging dusty and panting after a long day at work. We had the extra space in a barn on our rental property, so I volunteered to care for the chickens.

I loved each chicken. I bought them secondhand baby toys with flashing mirrors and crinkly, colourful dangling bits

from the recycle store. They pecked at my red toenail polish as I walked by, and this always made me laugh. Chloe sat
on an overturned bucket watching the baby chicks like Fern
in *Charlotte's Web*. The baby chicks kept her attention better
than any TV show. I had to drag her out of there when it was
time for dinner every night.

I let the birds out during the day to peck around the yard
within the large fish net I draped over the fence and barn so
that no raptors could swoop down to snatch them. The neighbours often had racoons stealing their chickens, and another
friend had her whole flock of pheasants murdered by a mink;
she cried when she saw their mangled bodies.

We tried a moveable chicken coop, but the chickens didn't
like being in a cage on the grassy lawn. I didn't blame them. I
made the fatal mistake of leaving the light on at night, so they
ate all night long. Some got too fat, and their legs couldn't
hold them up. There was one I named Stumpy (don't name
birds you are having for dinner). Rather than making him a
splint, we brought him to the water trough. In the end, we
decided his life was not a good one, sitting unhappily on the
grass with the human who was going to eat his brothers and
sisters. Rick took him out back and killed him.

"Stumpy!" I cried, after Rick had done the deed.

On the day the other birds were to be slaughtered, we
had put out a table outside and had a pot of boiling water.
Rick and Roger took turns killing the birds, and Cathy and I
plunged them into the hot water and plucked them. The men
then sliced them up, and we divided up the birds in big freezer
bags. I couldn't eat the chickens for a few months. The smell
of their feed was in their flesh, and it was too much.

WHEN THE girls wanted to go to Sandwell Beach and the soft
sloping sand at Lock Bay where we would swim through the

icy waves on a hot summer night, I was reminded of the sand at Winnipeg Beach. We spent whole days at Sandwell, the girls digging in the sand or finding logs to laboriously drag to the water to use as floats. After our swim, we'd race home and pull off our suits *thwickk, thwack*, damp, sandy towels over the faded fence boards, saggy bottoms mismatched or snagged on a rusty nail. The heat of the day's end warmed my damp behind as I breathed in the fragrance of the lemon balm engulfing an enormous round boulder that, to me, was a piece of garden art and not just a big rock.

All those days and weeks when Rick was away, and we were waiting for him to come home, we would watch Disney horse movies, yelling in mock excitement so our dog Stella would yelp in unison and make us laugh. We danced around the tiny patch of carpet we called the living room to '50s and '60s music, singing "Going to the Chapel" or "Surfin' Bird," using a hairbrush as a microphone. I danced barefoot on the strip of brown shag doing the mumbo. Dancing kept me sane on those long winter nights.

We didn't have cable, so to save money I rented DVDs like *Little House on the Prairie* from the library and cooked intricate meals that took a long time to prepare to keep from going mad. There was hardly a day that we weren't baking cupcakes or chocolate chip cookies. Later, I sat on the couch drinking Stella Artois and shoveling handfuls of cheesy nachos with waist-thickening guacamole into my mouth, stuffing down my loneliness. Sometimes I drank a whole bottle of red wine myself, stumbling blearily to bed after *Breakfast at Tiffany's,* weeping when Audrey Hepburn threw the cat out of the taxicab into the pouring rain.

Chloe and I played the card game Skip-Bo every night for an hour before bedtime. Hailey would lie in bed reading and rereading Harry Potter books. She was an aficionado who always won the Harry Potter trivia game and was drawn to a tall dark-haired English boy who had moved to the island.

We had huge fights to get Chloe to go to school; it almost broke me. I tried everything. We went to the school psychologist who suggested a chart with rewards. A no-nonsense friend said, "Just throw her in the car in her pajamas and then she'll listen." She never did get out of the car that day; I had to take her with me to my cleaning job, PJs and all.

Even our dog Stella missed the sound of Rick's noisy pickup truck with junk in the back rounding the bend at the corner of Ferne and Seymour. She just sighed and chewed at her toenails and fell asleep, her nose tucked into her tail. I resented looking after Stella, her expensive allergenic wheat-free dog food, her shedding, her upending of the neighbour's garbage bins full of diapers, her licking rotting compost bins before licking the kids' faces. She found a deer carcass, ate it, and then vomited it up on the living room floor. I put out an old sofa for her in the old horse barn and threw her a raw beef bone almost every day before I drove across the island to clean houses, hoping the bone would keep her occupied and that she wouldn't worm her way under the fence and get into trouble, which she almost always did. If I turned my back for a minute, she would eat the girls' breakfast. If I brought her in the car, the muffin in my purse would be eaten, plastic wrap and all. If I set out a bowl of Caesar salad, her snout would be in it in an instant.

Pets were the bane of my existence. I had to lock the cat in the barn at night with food and water and a little sleeping pillow or she woke me up every hour. If I put her outside, she found my window and scratched at it. If I let her in, she meowed to be let out. Some days I begged Rick to bring her to the SPCA. She puked every day unless I hand-fed her a few tablespoons of food at a time.

THERE IS nothing more humbling than knowing that the fifty bucks in your purse is the only fifty bucks you have for the next eight days. I knew exactly what payments were due and when, so if we were short, I would put twenty bucks into the account if necessary. I had many jobs; I taught children's crafts or was an election staffer when there was an election for fifteen dollars an hour. I painted pictures of sunflowers or pieces of driftwood with fish on them. If I was in a pinch, I borrowed the girl's birthday money they received from relatives. (We always paid them back.)

Everyone I knew sold jewelry or body products or collected honey or grew vegetables or made cards or knitted socks, all to sell. I wanted a job at the library but would have had to put in time on call, taking shifts anywhere from Nanaimo to Ladysmith. I was worried that the cost of extra child care and getting there would negate the higher wages. I did send in a resume now and then, with no results.

So, I cleaned houses for islanders, like the couple Esther and Eldon, who became good friends. Esther brought me gifts from her trip to Costa Rica and regifted me everything they didn't like from Christmas. She gave us handfuls of hand-me-downs: old Costco pajamas, T-shirts, raincoats, rubber boots and running shoes, carpets, bedding, mismatched cutlery, lamps, and an enormous TV that if tipped over would kill a small child or pet. Sometimes she would go into her lovely stainless-steel fridge and riffle around, fuming at the food that Eric bought and wasted. She put food in a Tupperware container and stuffed it into my cleaning basket as I walked out the door.

When I needed to save money for the girls' friends' birthday parties, they went through these items and found multi-coloured hippopotamus candles and glass pendants in the shape of lizards and paperweights with butterflies and all sorts of oddities to which I could never say no. It made us feel odd to always be on the receiving end of gift giving.

It seemed like our whole family life occurred in the house on five acres. I was cleaning Esther's house when Rick cut off the tip of his finger with an axle grinder attachment. I heard her clapping to get my attention and had to wind the snaking hose I used to vacuum her floors around my arm before turning it off to hear her. She said Rick had called, had hurt himself. I needed to go home right away.

HE WAS standing, waiting for us at the top of the gravel driveway with a giant towel around his bloody wound. We drove so fast we beat the ambulance to the clinic. The doctor gave him a shot to freeze the hand, and we were told to go to the hospital in Nanaimo for emergency surgery. Friends picked up the kids; another friend attended to Stella. At the hospital, a male nurse unwound his hand and blood squirted into his face, and he got mad, like Rick had done it on purpose. The surgeon said he would have to fuse the finger.

Later, after the surgery, we were back on the island, driving on the stretch of road islanders call the Tunnel. Rick looked concerned.

"The freezing is coming off," Rick said.

We had just driven off the last ferry and were about seven minutes from home.

"The pain's getting really bad," Rick said.

"Take the T-3s," I said.

"I already did," Rick said.

A MAJOR emergency is the worst thing to happen on an island when you know the last ferry has departed for the night and the Gabriola Medical Clinic will not be open until 9 AM the next morning. I felt a clenching in the pit of my stomach.

Normally, Rick has a high tolerance for pain. Once he hurt himself during softball practice, but he got up the next day and cycled to his job at the Nanaimo Shipyards. After work, he bicycled to Emergency. He discovered he had broken his ribs; the nurses were astonished he had cycled to the hospital. Another time, in the middle of the ocean, Rick ended up with a large gashing wound on his leg. He had to get stitched up with the help of whisky—some on the wound and the rest down his throat.

At home, I started pacing. I didn't know how to help.

"I might have to drink that bottle of vodka," Rick said in desperation.

"I have to lay down," I said.

The stress was too much for me. Looking back, I may have had my one and only bout of narcolepsy. A couple of hours later, Rick woke me up.

"I drank the whole bottle, but the pain is getting worse," he said.

"What can I do?"

"Call 911," he said.

I scrambled for the phone.

"They're asking, 'What is your pain level from one to ten?'" I said.

"Is about an eight," Rick said, slurring his words.

"I'm to keep you awake until the next ferry, and we'll get you back to emergency." I later learned, to get the ambulance service off hours, a person needed to have a pain level of ten.

"I'm really sleepy," Rick said.

"Get in the car. We're going for a drive." I bustled him out the door, thinking a change of scenery would keep him alert. As we looped around the island, I cast sideways glances at him.

"No sleeping! Stay awake!" I yelled if I saw his eyelids drooping. "It's only a couple of hours until the first ferry. Just hold on," I said, worried he would go into a coma. After a few laps around the island, with the music turned up loud and a steady stream of cold air funnelling into Rick's face, he made his plea.

"We can't go back to the Nanaimo hospital. They won't give me proper pain meds. Why didn't they give them to me after a major operation? They don't know me. They'll think I'm some sort of drug addict, especially after I drank so much vodka. Take me to Dr. Bosman, who knows me. Let's wait until the office is open over here."

I knew he was right. Although it was another four hours until the medical clinic opened. Could he last that long? When the local coffee shop opened, we were the first through the doors. I ordered Rick strong coffee to sober him up.

Finally, 9 AM rolled around. At the medical clinic, we were ushered into the exam room, and Dr. Bosman didn't hesitate to give Rick something to take away the pain; the muscles in his face went slack with relief.

That was one of the most stressful times of my life, at least I thought so then.

THE NEXT day, Esther came over to visit. Rick's bandaged hand was huge and bulky, like he had lost a whole hand and not just the tip of his finger. As a gruesome party trick, I would prod Rick to show small children the gnarled tip of his finger— warning about power tool safety. It made them scream and run away in fright.

Even though we both worked extra jobs, we never seemed to have enough spare cash. One year for Rick's birthday we went to the recycle store and I bought him an automatic wine opener for a dollar. That night his brother called him from Hawaii, and he talked about the giant marlin he had caught. I imagined its glassy eyes glinting in the sunlight. I'm sure

Rick wanted to be there with him. We were sitting around our battered dining table eating from Esther's mismatched plates and I suddenly worried that our small dinner for four with a cheap, poorly wrapped gift, may not be as magical as a hunt for marlin.

Later, I kissed the back of his thick neck and said, "I love you," like an incantation—isn't our love enough? But he was already asleep.

On the afternoons when he was home, and I got home early from cleaning houses we shared an "afternoon delight." Once we were interrupted by some Jehovah Witness canvassers, who knocked on our beautiful barnwood door. I tiptoed naked to peer out the window to see two people retreating down the looping gravel driveway, looking over piles of unused shoes curling with spider webs and dead flies around the window sill, unkempt piles of empty Stella Artois bottles and empty wine boxes.

But it wasn't all sweetness and light. When I was mad at Rick, I took down a painting I had made for him when we had been on a rare family trip to the Okanagan. The scene had him in his Hawaiian swim trunks, a fish tattoo winding around his large, freckled forearm, his orange hair and cheap black sunglasses against a backdrop of greenery. We drove our old gold Volvo stopping at campsites we had hoped would be empty but were instead packed with retired people in camper vans. The warm gentle breezes of summer had turned into hair-whipping weather. We finally found a campsite with a bit of protection and a lot of ducks. I always meant to finish the painting, but I never did. I put the painting of Rick under the bed because I was tired of being held hostage to love, holding down the fort during power outages and snowstorms.

In one instance, I had to walk through snowdrifts in my bathrobe while a friend's husband told me how to cover the well lines with a sleeping bag to keep them from freezing in the dead of night. The dog followed me as I walked alone through the wood-lined path to the little shed housing the well. I was proud I could turn off the pump and save the lines. The next day, the plumber showed up and took his time. I tried to signal with my eyes at the dirty pots and pans, covering up all the counters.

When Rick called every few days, I childishly wanted to punish him by not answering so he could know what it felt like. I couldn't let the phone ring more than a few times before I pounced on it, out of breath, terrified I'd miss even one short call. We talked about everything. I would wind the plastic cord around my fingers, telling him about the cat batting a mouse's head about, how Stella thought it was a toy, and got in on the game. I could hear the mice under my bed trying to nibble on my ear plugs, the ones I needed to help me sleep when Rick was home and drank too much wine and snored. Now he listened to me on the phone in a motel room on "blow days." When it was too stormy to work, they came into Prince Rupert.

RICK'S DIVE bag sits on the floor of our cramped bedroom, I stumble over it to get to the closet. It reeks of diesel fuel, cigarette smoke, and dampness. I fish out a favourite novel I asked him to read months ago. Now it is plump with moisture unread—unreadable now. The orange I packed five weeks before (to prevent scurvy) is now greenish white, stuck to an inside corner. A homemade licorice-scented bar of soap that he begged for sits unused and is squashed inside a plastic sandwich bag.

A special-order T-shirt that I bought him for Christmas, which I didn't want him to pack for work, is now rank, mixed in with his other work clothes. The T-shirt sports a giant bottle of Tabasco on the front, one of his favourite condiments. Rick blankets his food with the unnatural redness. I buy it monthly in large 500-mL glass bottles when he is home. When Rick is gone, Hailey, Chloe, and I slowly get accustomed to spicy foods because Rick is not home to use it up. We shake it onto our homemade pizza, our omelettes, our pasta.

One time as I gingerly picked out his laundry from the contents of the black, dank darkness, I found an unfinished pack of cigarettes and called him on it. We had quit smoking together when Chloe was born. Rick claimed it wasn't his, but the lie eventually grew too heavy, and he had to admit to it. This now explained why he was often cranky in the spring after he returned from his diving season. He had to requit smoking every summer. I often bring up his hidden smoking habit during fights. "How many other secrets are you keeping from me?"

When Rick leaves for work in September, at first I am glad for that extra space on the carpet. Soon my own junk migrates to that spot. I store my vacuum cleaner in this corner and stub my toe—and I wish it was his dive bag.

RICK'S PERSPECTIVE

When I first get home, I throw my dive bag full of my stinky work clothes in the corner of the room. I purposely forget about it because dealing with it requires that I think about work. I remember that I had brought that T-shirt Margot had given me. It is now dirty and stained, along with the rest of my clothes. I really don't care what I look like anchored up in a remote northern coastal location. I love my Tabasco T-shirt; the spice is like a salt addiction for me. The more I use, the more I need until I have to eat almost equal amounts of food and sauce. I know Margot had to special order it. I love this shirt because I know she really thought about finding it for me. I brought it along in my dive bag because wearing it makes me not so homesick. She doesn't know that it's hard for me to leave. Sometimes the homesickness feels unbearable.

ONE MORNING after I'd dropped the girls off at the school bus stop down the long, potholed Turkey Shoot Road, I came home to chop an armful of kindling and answered the telephone. I was surprised to hear the phone ring so early. It was my friend Kathy on the line.

She said, "I don't know how to tell you this, but I was driving to work this morning, and I heard on the radio that a diver drowned near Campbell River. Have you heard from Rick lately?"

My heart stopped. I couldn't breathe. The last time I had heard his voice, I was impatient. The dirty dishes had been overflowing from the morning's mad rush out the door, the house had been cold, and I had needed to bring in firewood. I had had a long evening making dinner and fighting with Chloe over homework. The night before, spelling practice had left me angry and shaking, so I was abrupt. Did I remember to say I love you?

I hadn't heard from Rick in ten days. I had the phone number of the wife of the man who owned the boat he was on. I dialed and asked if she knew where they were working— Campbell River, Port Hardy, Prince Rupert? They were dull pedestrian English names, I thought. I hardly paid attention when they moved areas. But she didn't know if that's where they were. I was sure it was him.

I had no one left to call. No options left. I wished I had a mother to call. Instead, I went to work. I drove back down that rutted gravel road with a carload of cleaning supplies to a ten-acre fenced property with a 3,000-square-foot house with hardwood floors, a grand piano, and a view of the ocean glittering past the treetops.

I cleaned the house for Suzanne, a real estate lawyer who worked in Calgary, and John, who was retired from a job with the Alberta government. I got to know everything about them, the intimate details of people's lives come to you as you are vacuuming up their dirt and the fur of their rambunctious dogs. Working as an island housekeeper, I knew what most people stored under their beds and who had moved to the spare bedroom. I overheard cancer scares, blood test results. I had been present when a dog got run over on a country road.

John knew something was wrong right away. We didn't talk about youth softball or basketball leagues or other small pleasantries. Instead, I got down to work. I tried not to think about Rick at the bottom of the sea, with fish pecking out his eyes. I brushed away the dead flies from around the window panes. I reached for spiderwebs. I got down on my hands and knees and washed that long wooden staircase, one step at a time. I wiped down the baseboards. I cleaned out the fridge. John handed me a bouquet of flowers from his garden when I was done. I understood then how some couples held their marriage together. I was, at that moment, trying to hold ours together myself.

I picked up a few things at the grocery store and headed home. I called Esther. She advised me that the RCMP would have notified me right away if the diver was Rick. They hadn't identified the body on the radio. I had to believe her.

I picked up Chloe from the school bus stop near Brickyard Beach. I instructed her to get started on dinner, spaghetti with Swiss chard. I drove back down Brickyard Hill to pick up Hailey, who was coming home on the next ferry. I saw an RCMP car drive up the hill past me. The sight of the patrol car incited my first panic attack. I was worried that they were on the way to my house to inform me of the bad news. But what if I was wrong? My head was muddled. I kept going.

After Hailey got in the car, I drove straight to the liquor store and bought a bottle of wine.

I STOOD in front of six people I see every day, and called Chloe from the phone behind the counter. I imagined two suited RCMP officers standing in the foyer, large and foreboding, as my daughter stood in the kitchen, afraid and alone. Instead, she was making dinner as instructed.

I drove home, trying not to be a blathering idiot because if the girls no longer had a father, they needed someone. It was Easter weekend. At home I pulled out the egg kits and blew the yolks out after making tiny pin pricks in the shells. We spent hours doing this at the coffee table Rick had made out of cheap wood and then roughed it up like he saw on a building show on TV.

We were invited to a friend's for turkey dinner on Saturday night. Afterward, we went home and watched Fred Astaire tap dance with Judy Garland. I guzzled more wine. Still no word from Rick.

The next night after the girls went to bed and I was alone, it dawned on me to try an internet search. I Googled "Diver drowned in Campbell River" and learned it was not a commercial diver, but a sport diver. I cried with relief.

The next morning, a man from one of the fish-packing boats called to say Rick was fine. His satellite phone wasn't working, but he was okay. The reality of his job hit me so hard that weekend that I don't think I ever fully recovered. Each time he called to say it was stormy, I said, "Take care," meaning your body, your soul, meaning come back alive. We need you. People loved to ask Rick about the dangers he encountered on the high seas, but I had to shut him down. He was no longer allowed to tell me when something dangerous occurred, which I knew deep down, was often.

THE LIGHT is flashing red on the answering machine, and I know instinctively it is Rick. I listen to the phrase he's been saying since the beginning of time: "It's me. I'm here, in the middle of nowhere."

Though I scoff at diver's superstitions—never open a can upside down on the boat; it's bad luck to have a woman on board; don't shave until all the fish have been caught—I always save one of his messages, just in case. If he drowns or is mistaken for a seal and is eaten by a killer whale, or his dive tender forgets to check for his air bubbles or forgets where he has dropped him, or the current has pulled him out to sea, or a sport fisherman has driven over his head, ignoring the red-and-white diver down flag, this message could be his last.

If the phone ever rings in the middle of the night, I always brace myself for tragedy. These thoughts surface in the dark of night, keeping me awake. I ask myself, *Is this a normal way to live? Would I choose this life again? Couldn't I have fallen in love with a banker, or a store manager who gets discounts, or a sushi chef who brings home tuna rolls from the restaurant every night? Would this imaginary husband enjoy going to karaoke night at the local Skol Pub? Would we have joined a bowling league or have season tickets to the ballet?*

Most days I am listing on choppy waves, like when I was pregnant on *The Buckaroo*, bracing myself against a window, the force of water about to crack. I am in turmoil, worried, and bitter, until Rick calls to say he is on his way home. I then feverishly clean the house, mop the floors, wash the bed-sheets. Hailey and Chloe are swept up in the whirlwind of excitement.

When he walks in the door, alive with his lopsided smile and chipped tooth, how can I not be grateful? He is in the middle of our nowhere now.

RICK'S EASY SPICY CHICKEN WINGS

This recipe makes the best chicken wings. Everyone loves them, and it takes hardly any time to prepare because the cheat is buying the two sauces and mixing them together.

Serves 2, if you eat alongside a large serving of Caesar salad (see page 93)

2 lbs chicken wings   Olive oil
   (about 10–12 wings)

For the Easy Sauce
½ cup of chicken and   ½ jar mild curry paste (such
   wings BBQ sauce   as Patak's)
                                  ½–1 tsp chili pepper flakes

Preheat oven to 425°F. Add chicken wings to rimmed baking sheet, and bake wings until browned. In a medium bowl, mix all the sauce ingredients together. Take wings out of the oven and coat in the sauce. Put back in the oven and bake for another 20 minutes.

ON HOT summer afternoons, you can almost always find me in a long-sleeved shirt wearing a mask and goggles in my cramped and stifling studio. I am stirring melted fats and lye in an attempt to turn the bubbling mass into tiny works of art. According to *Merriam Webster Dictionary,* saponification is the process of making soap or "the hydrolysis of a fat by an alkali with the formation of a soap and glycerol." The upside-down Es for pronunciation next to the entry read like an alien language—sə-ˌpän-ə-fə-ˈkā-shən—and it does feel other-worldly much of the time.

Many times a year, I make Pink Himalayan salt soap with lemongrass, lavender, and clary sage essential oils. The uplift-ing aroma invokes a sea goddess stepping glistening and regal from the ocean waves. Because of the salt, it must be cut within six hours of pouring or it will harden, crumble, and be ruined.

I make soap every other day from April to November. It is a big seller at our farmers' market. I pull on a pair of holey pants and a heavily perfumed- and oil-stained shirt, pull my hair back in a pink bandana, and put on my vapour mask. I wear closed-toed shoes and rubber gloves to guard against burning soap dripping on exposed skin. I work alone in my shop, stirring, until my hands cramp, pouring the soap into moulds, and covering the moulds with a thick sleeping bag while the soap sets. I emerge, goggles fogged and streaks of pale pink soap in my hair.

When I first dabbled in the craft, I used melt-and-pour glycerin soap, suspending flower blossoms, or tiny plastic toys, in clear round bars. Later, I adopted the labour-intensive cold process method. Each time I approach my shop, I take a gulp of fresh air before twisting the slippery handle and entering the space, which has a cloying mix of patchouli, pep-permint, clove, and Siberian fir needle—scents at war with each other in this small space. Boxes of metal salve tins rain down on my head as I grasp for items on the top shelves. I can only make forty bars at a time, so between batches, I traipse twelve paces across the driveway to wash the soap moulds and utensils in our kitchen sink.

I once reveled in the magic of it, the way the slippery oils were transformed through chemistry into fragrant and natu-ral gifts. People are always stopping me in the street to say, "I thought of you in the shower today." Each bar is as unique as a snowflake, not uniform and factory perfect. Starfish drape over each rectangle, an artist's model posed seductively across a soapy divan.

Rick make all my starfish molds as well as wooden displays made from driftwood, some sagging precariously or tipping over and denting my soap. Once, in a gust of wind, one of his signs almost knocked me out. This was all the more embarrassing when an elderly woman who witnessed it told me to sit down and said, "How many fingers am I holding up?" and then "You should get your husband to fix that sign."

Sometimes I weep into the cauldron, the pain of missing Rick too much, or for the loss of holidays and special occasions that we might have spent together. When I sob into my batch of soap, I think of Tita in *Like Water for Chocolate*, a woman distraught as she makes the wedding cake for the man she loves, but who is marrying her sister. She cries into the batter and later the wedding guests feel her intense longing and sadness when they bite into the cake.

Sharing a kitchen with a gourmet-food making family while running a one-woman soap operation is no easy feat. Do these feelings of frustration and desperation leach into my bars and infect my customers while they are sliding it innocently over their bodies? Do they sense my ennui? I need the hot running water and a clean empty sink in our kitchen, only to find that I have to fend off a hungry family member trying to make themselves a meal using the counter space I had meticulously cleaned. Sometimes Rick walks in from his workshop, sawdust flying from his shoulders, to make kombucha or kimchi and numerous sauces from scratch, messy things that splatter.

I became a soapmaker to earn extra income, but it has become a part of my identity. As the principal of Starfish Soap Company, I have presided over the table at our farmers' market, rain or shine. I sell primarily to tourists to Gabriola Island, but I have a loyal, local fan base, too. When I first started out, Marin, a jewelry maker, and I would often be the first ones in line for drop-in spots. She had a baby in tow; I often had Chloe. Every Saturday I would set up, under the cool shade of a tree with Chloe chewing on my shoulder from her perch on my back while Hailey ran wild in a stained tie-dye dress on her way to a tree limb, often getting stuck and crying for me to help her down.

Next to me, vendors sell homemade popsicles, or hand painted rocks, or vinegar, or pies/chocolate scones/cinnamon buns/focaccia bread, or strawberries and refrigerator magnets. Some have droned on about how they cooked their eggs in the morning until my eyes glazed over. The pre-sale conversations have been wide-ranging. Some have told me about their rashes in the oddest places. Some have had grating laughs. Some have ooh and ahhhed over the girls' greeting cards, sold for a dollar each.

When the girls were younger, after we would get home, I would unload the heavy boxes of soap to fit everyone in for our trip to the beach. The next morning, I would reload the car with my boxes of soap to sell at the south end of the island, and then I would do it all over again, Chloe used to help me set up and later would patiently play on the sloping grass lawn, or would count dragonflies. Sometimes the wind would tunnel through from the water, and we would hang on tight to the corners of the tent, hoping it wouldn't rain.

I admit to daydreaming about a different future, a time when I will no longer need to spend hours inside my dark shop, when the birds outside are swooping among the arbutus inviting me to the beach. I dream about swimming in the fragrant depths of the ocean only to emerge and stride onto the shore, wind ruffling my hair as I step over starfish, and into my new life.

STARFISH SOAP COMPANY'S FAMOUS PINK HIMALAYAN SALT BARS

Measure everything on a scale before beginning. Wear proper protective gear. See my soap blog (washrinserepeatdot. wordpress.com) for basic soap-making instructions.

Oils

1,875 g coconut oil (76 Degree)

126 g aloe butter
160 g cocoa butter
400 g olive oil (pomace)

Lye solution

352 g lye (sodium hydroxide)

973 g water (reverse osmosis)

Salt & clay mixture

60 g French pink clay

1,000 g finely ground pink Himalayan salt

Essential oils

42 g lavender essential oil
42 g lemongrass essential oil

42 g clary sage essential oil

Melt the coconut oil, aloe butter, and cocoa butter in your soap pot until liquid, then mix in the olive oil and set aside to cool to 100 degrees.

While the oils are melting, gear up and pour your lye crystals into your pre-measured water in a water container with a lid. Stir in a safe place away from children and pets and wear a mask and eye protection. Let the lye/water mixture cool down to 100 degrees before stirring into your oils.

Mix the French pink clay into the pink Himalayan salt. Stir well to get out the clumps. Stir the essential oils into the salt/clay mixture and set aside.

Grease mould and measure and cut waxed paper to place on top of your soap. Have a couple of thick towels or an old sleeping bag ready to insulate your soap.

Check temperatures of both melted oils and lye/water solution. When they are both at 100°F, it is time to stir up your soap. With protective gear on, mix the melted oils with the lye/water solution for 5 minutes by hand. Use a stick blender for 1 minute, and then stir for 1 minute by hand. Alternate the stirring until the mixture has emulsified or has thickened and has come to trace. Stir in the salt/essential oil/clay mixture.

Pour into soap mold. Cover with waxed paper and sleeping bag or towels.

Cut salt soap after about 6–7 hours. Set salt soap bars in a moisture-free area to cure for 4–6 weeks.

11

RED SKY AT NIGHT

"E VERYTHING IN the ocean reminds me of sex," Rick said as he pulled out a mangled geoduck clam from a Styrofoam cooler. Geoducks are normally too valuable for him to bring home to eat, but its broken shell had rendered it unsaleable. Pacific geoducks, pronounced, goo-ee-ducks, are giant burrowing clams with long necks sprouting out of white hard shells. When you hold one in your hands, it is like you are cradling a giant horse's penis. I raised my eyebrows when Rick held it between his legs and smiled his lopsided smile. There must be a million photos of geoduck divers, dangling one of these clams between their legs, a goofy grin on their faces.

Earlier that summer, much to my chagrin, Rick had gotten a job at a geoduck farm near Savoury Island, north of Powell River on the Sunshine Coast. The money was too good to pass up—three hundred dollars a day—a lot more than he could make laying hardwood floors on aching knees. I cried when I heard he wouldn't be home after a long winter of waiting. I kept telling myself, *I can make it until the spring; I can make it. It's only another couple of months, a few more weeks, a couple more days . . .* I begged him to try to find work on the island for the summer.

"I need you! The girls need you here!" I cried.

But he was adamant.

To Rick, getting a job on a geoduck boat was like the Holy Grail of dive jobs. Pacific geoduck clams went for about fourteen dollars a pound, compared to one dollar a pound for sea urchins. The coveted jobs usually went to fishermen's sons and close family members, but this time Rick would be working with his old diver friend, Tony Mulhall, on *The Kathron*.

Geoducks are found forty to sixty feet underwater. Divers locate them by searching for "the show"—tell-tale circles in the sand. If none appear, a diver throws a five-pound lead ball, called a cannonball, normally used for sport fishing or trolling for salmon, into the water. When the ball hits the bottom, the clams sink and create circular air holes as they burrow.

Rick's job was to purge the wild geoducks from their hiding spots under the mud and sand. He would get air from a long hose connected to the surface, not from heavy oxygen tanks. He blasted the clams using a high-pressure water hose with a nozzle, called a stinger. Then he stuck his arm into the hole, right up to his shoulder, to pluck it out.

Every morning they left the dock at 6 AM to drive *The Kathron* three hours to reach the designated spot. This left them just enough time to collect three cages of geoducks and drive back. On the boat when they got hungry, Tony and Rick ate raw broken clams, sliced from the tip of a knife. But after their workdays, they would sit on lawn chairs and drink Lucky beer.

Back on Gabriola, the skies were filled with brilliant reds and pinks: *Red sky at night, sailor's delight*. Rick called me to say that if the weather was that beautiful, he would even go swimming when he returned. I reminded him of our upcoming camping trip to Bamfield with our friends Ken and Kathy Gurr and their daughters Anya and Mara.

It was the middle of August when we packed up our pie irons and camping gear in the back of the gold Volvo. The

Gurr family and us both billeted our dogs (they had a Jack Russell) for the week with an islander named Judy, who boarded them in her old barn. Then we headed out. Stella had a habit of waking us whenever she heard rustling in the forest. She would stuff her snout into the tent zipper and wiggle outside, barking hysterically. We had to chase after her in the dark, tripping over roots, while calling out in a hushed voice, so as to not to not wake other campers.

We caught the early morning ferry to Nanaimo and made stops, first at Starbucks and later for burgers, then we drove up-island along the winding, potholed road to Bamfield. Chloe was eleven and Hailey was fifteen. They both loved leaving the island for a holiday, even a short one. Hailey worked every weekend at Mad Rona's Coffee shop as a barista, saving money for a trip to Peru.

At the Pachena Bay Campground, we cooked hot, made-to-order grilled pizza sandwiches, over the campfire, with pie irons, heavy, hand-held panini presses. We filled them with fancy Havarti cheese and deli meat folded between thick slices of buttered bread. We added olives and pasta sauce and mushrooms and onions.

We hiked the forest trail to Keeha Beach and visited the Bamfield Marine Sciences Centre to walk off the excess. Hikers emerged from the West Coast trailhead solemn-faced and filthy.

On our last day at the campground, we made a sauna on the beach from long pieces of driftwood and a plastic tarp by pouring water over rocks from our beach fire. It rains in Bamfield one hundred and ninety days of the year, so all things considered the weather had cooperated.

Around the campfire, we drank beer as Rick told stories about whales bumping the side of the boat n the night and jolting him awake with their loud exhales. The next day, as we wandered along the beach, we witnessed a single humpback in the shallow ocean swells. Rick waded out in the water up to his chest about one hundred metres from the shore. We weren't sure what the whale was doing so close to the beach. At first, we thought it was going to rub its body along the rocks, but Rick thought it may have been feasting on something. I was sure it wanted to feast on us, so I yelled at Rick to come back. I was reminded of the time he had grabbed a bear that was swimming by his boat. He was always trying to get near wildlife, couldn't control himself.

On the way back to Gabriola, both tires popped on the rough road, and we had to stop at a garage in Port Alberni to get them repaired. Every holiday ended with our car breaking down; we almost expected it. On our last camping trip our van was totaled by a kid on a dirt bike. He got up and fled the scene. We had to rent a car to get back home and only got a pittance from our insurance.

Once home, we hung colourful boat floats from Keeha Beach on our deer fence, as tokens of a trip stolen from the geoducks and the gods of weather, one red sky at a time.

WHEN I landed at Winnipeg International Airport, it all came rushing back, all the times I'd left, all the times my daughter had hung from my hip while I cried and waved goodbye to my Little Baba. I cried because I realized again, that Winnipeg was no longer my home.

I chose to raise my family away from Winnipeg's grueling heat and swarms of mosquitoes, cheaper housing, and crumbling roads, crippled by construction. Whenever I flew across the country to visit the dwindling stock of relatives there, the city always greeted me with these hallmarks.

This trip was different. This time I was here to visit my old friends Roxanne and Corinne. I travelled with a dusty backpack, borrowed from Hailey after her trip to Peru. I was embarrassed when the talkative female airport security guard found Hailey's trash in a hidden pocket: a crumpled tube of toothpaste, a tampon, a shriveled tea bag, and a granola bar wrapper.

Roxanne picked me up in her Pontiac with the wide, comfortable leather seats. She got a deal from her boyfriend, though the transmission had seen better days. We were on our way to Corinne's cottage in Lake of the Woods. Her cabin has granite countertops and is four times larger than my house.

Before we left Winnipeg, I told Roxanne I wanted to drive by my childhood home. "It won't take long; I just want to check out the neighbourhood."

On the way, we passed Holy Trinity Orthodox Church and its onion-shaped domes. We passed Cropo Funeral Chapel, where we held the services first for my mother and then for Little Baba.

We drove by the local flower shop that used to be Karen's but must have been purchased by someone named Sonya. The Salisbury House restaurant's red-peaked roof reminded me where my baba and I ate hot dogs with plain mustard. She only had a few teeth left and had to chew carefully. We drove past the store where the shopkeeper used to show neighbourhood kids his concentration camp tattoo before I knew what it meant. During the summer I visited this store daily, blackening my bare feet to buy Pixy Stix, cardboard straws filled with red powdered sugar that stained my tongue.

The Pontiac turned down a familiar street lined with elm trees. McAdam Avenue is lined with two-storey Cape Cod houses, fronted by tiny patches of green lawn. All the living is done in the backyards, where fences hide the clotheslines, lawns are converted into small garden plots, and badminton nets sag from overuse. It began to rain as soon as we stepped out of the car. I wished I had worn a heavier sweater.

Roxanne parked too close to the house. I didn't want to see Ronald, my mother's widower. After the court battle, Ronald told Tanya and me he never wanted to hear from us again, which was fine by us. The driveway was empty, so we walked on by.

I could see from across the street that there was a black iron knocker on the front door, the one my mother picked out in the '70s. It was in the shape of a wolf's head, a symbol of power and strength. It differentiated the house from all the others; something still remained of her, something solid. She always had good and lasting taste.

A bright orange clump of marigolds growing along the driveway reminded me that my mother always grew them. It made me absurdly happy to see them. My mother had the fir tree cut down years ago. She had said she didn't like us tracking in the pine needles. I had converted its stump to an uneven table, and dragged it from house to house but eventually abandoned it in an alleyway. I never could let things—or people—go.

A month ago, I had searched for my old family home using Google Maps. I peered down from the clouds into my old backyard to see what still might remain of my childhood. Gone were my mother's prized lilac bushes, their fragrant flowers often gracing a vase on our dining room table. I could almost smell the sweet dillweed towering against the garage and the vegetable garden where I picked tomatoes, which we ate quartered and drowned in white vinegar and salt and pepper.

I was getting cold now, the rain having soaked through my thin sweater and sandals. I looked back at the house and was surprised to see Ronald in his mid-seventies, retired, and wondering who was parked in front of the house.

I grabbed Roxanne's arm and told her not to look back. "He's there. Looking out the door."

"Do you want me to get the car?" she asked.

"Yes, I can't let him see me."

I waited in the cold rain, ashamed. I remembered his drunken rants. The fights they had at the dining room table at dinner, Tanya and I taking our plates to the basement "dungeon" to finish eating. We balanced our meals on our laps as we watched TV, turning it up to block out their escalating voices.

I only stood up to him once, after I flew in from BC for my mother's last days and funeral. It was a cold day in February, the kind of day that makes your lungs hurt. I stood in the living room. It was the last in a long line of uncomfortable family meetings.

"How long are you going to stay? You can't stay here without paying rent."

I raised my voice for the first and last time. "I have had enough. I came here for my mother's funeral. For her. I am packing up today and I am taking Tanya with me." He looked shocked. I had never raised my voice before to him. I felt powerful for the first time.

Roxanne's car pulled up to the corner where I was standing. I hesitated before I climbed in. *I should turn around, go back to the house, my mother's house,* I thought. *I should walk right up those three steps and bash that wolf's head until Ronald comes out so I can tell him the house doesn't belong to him. My mother would do it; she would never give up.*

I climbed into the car seat.

"Are you okay?" Roxanne asked.

"I'm fine."

Roxy maneuvered back onto Main Street, and we headed for the cabin. We sped past the Tim Horton's where I worked at age sixteen, hating the itchy brown polyester uniform and the cigarette smoke you could taste in the donuts.

Outside the city, we passed a faded sign that said, REPORT POACHERS. The clouds parted and the hot sun streamed through the windshield. I regretted not visiting my mother's grave. I put on my sunglasses and swallowed pain, stared straight down the road as we careened out of town, the clumps of thin aspens a blur of green as we headed farther and farther away.

MY RIGHT hand was stained and ripped to shreds. I tried to ignore the pulsing of an insect bite on my wrist as I stopped briefly to pick burrs from my pant leg. I appreciated the sugary sweetness in the air as I waded deeper into the bush, balancing the stockpot on my hip. I headed farther away from my trusty gold Volvo, parked next to a set of rural mailboxes where I normally picked Chloe up from the school bus. Once Tanya had sent us Purdys chocolates for Hailey's birthday, but by the time we collected the package, the chocolate had melted into a puddle. And then there was the time Hailey opened up a letter addressed to me that looked official, and before she could read it, the wind whisked the sheaf of paper out of her hands like an escaped bird, never to be seen again. We both looked at each other with surprise.

"That's okay." I said, "Although, I hope it wasn't a million-dollar cheque in my name."

On this particular morning, I wore the protective gear of a person going to war—war against the thorns, the wasps, the bees, the thistles, the rising cost of our family grocery bill. I grasped the pot handles tightly to push down the vines and leaned in towards the ripe berries unnoticed by other pickers earlier in the day. Deer had trampled pathways to the branches, rearing up on their hind legs to get at the ripe berries waving tantalizingly off the top stalks. This popular island patch across from Brickyard Beach always has a lot of competition, human and otherwise, but somehow there are always enough to go around.

I once witnessed a man driving his tractor along the side of the road with his wife. He hoisted her high in the bucket to get at the good berries. I have seen people harvest berries with ladders or even a shield made of plywood and rope. If you tell islanders you are picking "near Brickyard," they know it's the large marshy area across from the old brick factory, above a rocky stretch of beach, littered with broken red bricks, the words *Dominion* pressed into their sides. They are prized by gardeners who collect them to line their flower beds. It is at this beach that we dig for clams and hunt for oysters if there's no red tide (algae blooms).

My friend Kathy and I liked to pick here together, moving from bush to bush, carefully avoiding the patch of thistles as we walked and talked, fingers in motion.

"Rick has spent thousands of dollars—money we don't have—building his boat. When I complained, he replied, 'Without my boat, I have nothing.' What does that mean, he has nothing? What are we?"

"Ken cut down my rose bush," Kathy said. "Why would he do such a thing?"

Berry picking is therapeutic.

Once Kathy hunted in her husband's closet for an old shirt to protect my arms when we decided on an impromptu foray into the patch.

"Ken never wears this. It has long sleeves so will be fine," she said.

Sometimes the thorns thrash your forearms or stain your clothes, right down to your underpants.

Later, Kathy told me, "Ken said that we ruined his one good shirt."

I had returned it purple and shredded at the cuffs.

"I never saw you wear it. Not once," Kathy said in defence to her husband.

"Well, yeah, because it's my *good* shirt," Ken replied.

On this morning, I was with Rick because I was not talking to Kathy. He knew without my saying so that I missed her.

"You should call her," he said gently.

THERE WAS a time when I called Kathy every evening to chat. But talking to her had become too painful. I couldn't stop comparing our families. Kathy's husband, Ken, is always there for his family, every night, every holiday. I don't think they've gone more than a few days apart. Instead of Rick's freckled body on the bed beside me, our stinky dog slouched next to me to chew her toenails.

I relied on Kathy to invite us to Easter dinners or Thanksgiving feasts. Chloe only liked Kathy's stuffing because it was more familiar than Rick's. Kathy would spend all day in her tiny kitchen making scalloped potatoes, a baked ham, homemade rolls, Brussels sprouts, cooking up dairy-free options for Chloe's food allergies. Ken called the kids "Hailey-Louise" and "Chlo-Chlo" in a funny voice to amuse us. I sat at their wooden dining table sipping wine, and Rick would call there from his satellite phone; their number is only two digits off of ours. Sometimes I felt that I couldn't stand their kindness one more minute.

One night Kathy called me on it. "You are a very demanding friend."

I felt hurt, but I knew it was true. I couldn't bear to be so needy. My pride was hurt. I was determined not to be a burden. So, I stopped calling her, and when I saw her at book club, I turned to talk to someone else across the table, ignoring the hurt in her eyes.

RICK IS a fast picker, all business, diving deep into a black-berry patch, heedless of the thorns. I punched tiny holes on either side of a plastic ice cream bucket and hung a purple yarn handle around his neck to free up his hands. He moved like a bear; the branches cracked under the weight of his body.

When there was a cougar sighting in the area, I brought Stella along in the mornings when it was cooler. I lured her with fat juicy berries so she would follow me. She caught anything we threw her way. She was really too old to defend me from cougars, but she distracted me from thinking about being attacked.

Rick is not only a trained hunter and a fast gatherer. On this day, he helped me pick pale pink wild rose petals for a soap recipe I make once a year in June, filling Ziploc bags in half the time it takes me. Rick did not bother to change his clothes or select proper shoes for our outing. Once he climbed a tropical mountain in bare feet. He wore his paint-splotched Crocs to pick berries, which seemed dangerous given the thorns, but when I told him to be careful, he waved me off.

"I'm tough," he said.

Ahead, he pointed out the dragonflies and swallows, joy-fully sweeping the sky for bugs. I felt the same way. If I came here every night, we'd have enough berries for the year. Rick was plotting to stir up a spicy jalapeño blackberry jam, and I wanted to bake a pie. From our yearly efforts, I usually had enough for a blackberry smoothie every day, blended with handfuls of kale from the garden.

Rick had made a spicy clam chowder the night before, and when we returned the shells to the beach, he found a sprig of sea asparagus for that day's dinner.

The Indigenous people on Gabriola had clam beds at El Verano, where sport fishermen and Mudgekins (residents from Mudge Island) now pull their boats up onto the natural sloping boat launch. There is no ferry to Mudge, no stores. Their main means of moving across their island is with a handful of dilapidated vehicles that are barged over.

I have only been there a handful of times, to sell soap for their annual fire department fundraiser. A man with deep creases in his tanned face picked up Chloe and me and all my hodgepodge of plastic bins of soap and threw them into the back of his pickup.

He said, "The day they build a bridge is the day I pull out my gun. Just let them try it."

The idea of building a bridge across Mudge to Gabriola has inspired great debate and Mudgekins are clearly dead set against it.

Past the rippling waters around Mudge Island, I could see the chugging smokestacks from the pulp mill, Harmac, near Nanaimo, working overtime. Some days the air is thick with the stink of it.

While Rick and I were berry picking that day, the wind caught the sugary sweetness that wafted up in the heat. I heard the hum of the electric power lines overhead, contaminating the berries with radiation. I picked on.

AT HOME, I looked up the term "blackberry plant" on the internet and was disappointed to learn that it is an invasive species called the Himalayan blackberry, prolific in southern BC. They are the "thugs of the plant world," choking out natural plants, causing soil erosion and flooding. Yet I am grateful for this plant; I fill my freezer and feed my family blackberries. My neighbours too make blackberry rhubarb pie, rolling out pie dough, dipping up cups of white grainy sugar.

I love the word "wildcraft"; uttering it makes me feel clever and witchy. I imagine crawling among the underbrush, inhaling the sweet scent of the rotting berries. I imagine a dainty mouse feasting at night on the berries that slipped from my stained fingers, birds getting tipsy from the fermented berries at the end of the season.

I have an unfinished bottle of blackberry wine that my sister Tanya brought over, during one of her rare visits to Gabriola. Its slender bottle sports a picture of a half-naked wine goddess, but it is too sweet to drink more than one glass. I prefer a cold beer at night.

ON SUNDAYS at the Silva Bay Market, I often sat next to May, a Thai lady of indeterminate age whom I have known for a long time. May would pick blackberries and sold them to people who did not want to go to the trouble of collecting them. She lives close to Kathy and Ken, in a trailer on a sunny hillside. The property overflows with thornless blackberries, apple and pear trees, vining cucumbers, and raised vegetable beds. I suspect she may have been a mail order bride. Her husband has at least ten years and a couple of feet on her. He would pick her up from the market in their beat-up van. May was a regular at the market, selling pungent bouquets of Thai basil or tomato plant starts. For the four hours at the market, May and I would sit in the cool wind, blankets wrapped around our shoulders as we waited for sales. May's stories would go something like this:

"I have a daughter. She comes to visit. She's the good daughter." I nodded my head. "The bad daughter, she doesn't visit. He lose his penis, see? Like this." She made a chomping motion with her teeth, like she was biting off a piece of cucumber.

I nodded and wondered if I should smile or look concerned.

"Wow" was all I could think of to say, wishing I had paid closer attention to the thread of her story.

May asked me to join her berry picking, because she too had heard that a cougar was skulking around our side of the island, but I didn't join her. Instead, when I saw her moped at the side of the road, my competitive nature kicked in. I dropped the girls off at soccer practice, raced home and changed into my stained berry-picking pants from the recycling depot, drove down Brickyard Hill, and waged war.

CLAM CHOWDER

The fun part of this recipe is digging for the clams. I normally watch from the sidelines as Rick does all the hard work. We collect clams and oysters from Brickyard Beach, across from our blackberry-picking patch. What could be better than free food, wildcrafted on the shore?

If you are collecting the clams yourself, make sure you have a fishing licence and check to see how many clams you can legally harvest. After collecting the clams, set them in a cool place and keep them in sea water. Pour in 2 cups of oatmeal and leave them overnight. This will degrit the clams, making them more palatable to eat. For fresh clams, boil them in water or steam them in a large pot until they open their shells.

Makes 8–12 servings

25–30 fresh clams, scrubbed, and steamed or boiled and removed from their shells or 3 (6 ½ oz) cans of clams
4 pieces bacon or pancetta
2–4 garlic cloves

1 onion, diced
4 celery stalks
3 Tbsp butter
3 Tbsp flour
½ cup dry white wine
4 cups chicken broth
1 lb (6 medium-size) potatoes with skin on, cut into ½-inch squares

Bay leaf

¼ tsp ground thyme

2 tsp Hungarian paprika

½ tsp freshly ground
    black pepper

½ –1 tsp hot chili flakes

2½ cups heavy cream
    (18%)

1 can (250-mL) creamed
    corn

Roughly chop the clams in a food processor and set aside. Next, cook the bacon in a heavy saucepan. Save a tablespoon of the grease and fry the garlic, onions, and celery in it until soft and translucent. Remove vegetables to a bowl and set aside. Next add butter and of flour to pan over medium heat to make a roux. When mixture has darkened, add white wine to deglaze the pan, and then add the vegetables, the chicken stock and the cut-up potatoes. Next, add the bay leaf and spices (thyme, paprika, pepper, and chili flakes). Bring mixture to a boil. Cook over medium heat until the potatoes are soft, stirring occasionally with a wooden spoon. Next stir in cream and the can of creamed corn and bring back up to a gentle boil. This is when you stir in the clams. Keep at a low boil for 2 minutes.

Take out bay leaf. Serve the clam chowder with a slab of fresh bread.

12

CLEANING UP
A STORM

EVERY WEEKDAY morning, I dropped the girls off at the ferry for their trek across the ocean to high school in Nanaimo, and I drove across the island to my various cleaning jobs. The back of the Volvo was stuffed to the brim with mops, a pail, and my blue plastic laundry basket filled with a mass of laundered rags, Murphy Oil Soap, Vim bleach cleaner—a hodgepodge of things to spray, shine, sanitize, and disinfect.

Cleaning was one of the few well-paying jobs for women on the island, and an improvement over cashier jobs at Village Food Market or the pharmacy. Another big draw was that I could make my own hours to accommodate the girls and shuttling them around on an island where everything was spread out with no public transit. Men on the island were carpenters, boat builders, or drywallers. If they had a truck, they hauled garbage to Nanaimo for a fee or got a job working on the ferry crew. Rick had signed up for the non-refundable training courses—a necessary step in the application process to work for BC Ferries—but a better dive job on a better boat always kiboshed it.

I was worried that Rick and I had really broken up for good, that our time apart had finally taken its toll. Rick had called me the night before to say, "That's it. I set you free."

I had been cranky that he was going to be away for another week. *It was the waiting that was going to kill me,* I thought.

"What do you mean? You can't do this. I love you! Don't hang up!" I had said.

AFTER A sleepless night, I was bleary-eyed. I made Mason jars with layers of muesli, sliced strawberries, and yogurt, Martha Stewart–style, and handed the girls each a spoon. As I drove them to the 7:35 AM ferry, I hoped my face didn't give away the storm inside, the worry that I would have to tell them that their parents were separating.

I hoped that moving my body would give me reprieve from replaying last night's phone call. It was a Wednesday, which meant that I needed to head over to clean Esther's house. As usual, I let myself in without knocking. I could hardly hide my misery as I set the laundry basket at my feet.

"I think it's really over," I told her. "Rick called last night to end it. I'm so tired. I need something to help me sleep. Do you have anything?"

She rooted around her bathroom shelves and found a box of Sudafed.

"What will I do?" I said, taking the package for later.

"You'll be okay," she said.

It was not lost on us that I didn't have a mother to call.

I VIGOROUSLY vacuumed the floors and area rugs, mopped the hardwood floor, dusted the sideboards, and cleaned the bathrooms. I energetically wiped down the shower doors, my body on autopilot. After cleaning this house for close to eight years, I knew every corner of it. I knew where to find a spider web that popped up weekly in the corner of the kitchen, and where the cat liked to hide her wretched furballs.

After a few hours of cleaning up a storm, I began to feel optimistic. I told Esther I was considering returning to school, maybe to learn something practical, like nursing. I would be able to make it on my own with a new career, untangled from Rick at last. He had done me a favour by setting me free. Although I was grasping. I couldn't imagine plunging a needle into someone's flesh. Esther encouraged me; helping people was what she lived for.

WEEKS AGO, I had sensed that things were getting worse. I had made an appointment with Dr. Bosman because my heart had started racing. I told him I couldn't sleep, and he prescribed calming walks. So, after midnight, I had headed out into the darkness, no streetlights, just bats flying erratically, and the crunch of gravel on a deserted street. I walked down the road, circling around the large puddle that pooled in a corner of our driveway. I wandered around in my nubby blue bathrobe, with a daughter on each arm. When we were together, it felt like we were on a late-night adventure, instead of on a walk to ease my nerves, to calm my racing heart.

I got an ultrasound to make sure that the pain in my left side was not ovarian cancer. I got my heart tested, vials of blood drawn and analyzed. Dr. Bosman said I was illness-free. I went on an elimination diet and lost forty pounds. I quit drinking beer, stopped eating dairy, sugar, and carbs. I looked great but couldn't stop crying. I cinched in my pants rather than buying new ones, convinced I'd regain the weight. Why spend money on new pants if I might grow out of them?

For Chloe's thirteen birthday party, I had booked the local hair salon to do her friends' hair and nails as a kind of salon party. I rushed to the tiny bathroom and sat doubled over in pain from that morning's procedure where I was laid out on a table and injected with dye that would show in photos of my looping intestines, but I didn't say a word. I was determined not to ruin Chloe's special day.

ONE OF the first people I called after Rick set me free was my old friend Roxanne in Winnipeg. I wept to her on the phone. A few days later, a package from her miraculously arrived.

I was taking Chloe to her weekly dance lesson in Nanaimo, and I sat on the ferry reading her note. I held it close, feeling the love through her kind words. Roxanne had sent me a cheque for five hundred dollars. She recommended that I buy myself something nice, so I did. I dropped Chloe at Harbour Dance and headed to the secondhand shop where I bought myself a sweater and a funky hat. This was a real treat because I rarely spent any extra money on myself. Back at home, I read the label in my new hat and discovered the company was called Roxy. I felt this was a sign—I wasn't alone in the world.

Of course, I wasn't alone. Later that night, Hailey and Chloe sat next to me on the couch—one daughter on each side to hold me up. I kept the curtains closed, like I was ashamed the world would find out that I had failed in love. I disconnected the landline from the wall. I sipped a beer to help calm me.

"Why not talk to Dad? What good will it do to unplug the phone?" Hailey asked.

"I want him to worry a little," I admitted.

I was tired of Rick knowing that I was always at home waiting for his call, ready to pounce on the first ring. I wanted to apply the pressure of uncertainty. I was afraid if I answered, I might beg him to reconsider. I might lie and say I would learn to be stronger, agree that a long-distance relationship was not so bad after all. I would get used to it.

Hailey, at age seventeen, was a voracious romance novel reader. She didn't believe my method of cutting off communication was the proper route back to love.

"It will work," I assured my daughters. My hands shook as the warm beer slid down my throat. The girls rubbed my shoulders and petted my arms.

It took Rick four days to make it back home. I had the only working vehicle in the family. I needed to haul my cleaning gear, drive the girls to the ferry terminal to go to school, travel back and forth on the ferry when we needed supplies in Nanaimo, and sell soap at the market on the weekends. I knew it would be a tough trek for Rick to return without proper transportation.

Rick pulled up in a taxi. He never had to call a cab before because I was always there to pick him up from his work trips. I would arrive at the ferry, late at night in my pajamas, bare feet shoved into soap-stained shoes. When the kids were little, I would haul them out of bed, half-asleep, heavy as sacks of potatoes, and dump them in their car seats to drive across the island to meet Rick's ferry. I didn't mind the inconvenience.

This time things were different. I didn't smile as I stood blocking the doorway. I was about to go for a walk down the trail at the end of Wild Cherry Terrace.

Rick dropped his heavy dive bag on the foyer floor. "You look pretty," he said, noticing my new gray hat.

I wanted to stay mad, but as soon as I saw his freckled face, I forgot all the pain. I forgot all those nights that I was certain loneliness would kill me. I let him envelope me into his strong arms. I put my nose in the crease of his neck and wept with relief.

We made promises we wouldn't keep. He would take dive jobs closer to home; I would stop pressuring him. I would find time to do something for myself. I would go back to school. Maybe I would learn to write.

A FEW days after Rick had gone back to work, I was upbeat. I watched *How I Met Your Mother* and *The Big Bang Theory* with Hailey and Chloe. I created new soap recipes with apricot kernel oil and mango butter. But it wasn't long before the old refrain started playing in my head: *This waiting is too much. These long trips are too much to bear. Why can't he get a job closer to home? Doesn't he love us enough to change?*

At night, sadness swept over me, and the only thing that calmed me was practicing typing on the computer. All the jobs I had seen posted online were office administrator jobs. I imagined we were a different kind of family—the kind who worked Monday to Friday, had regular paycheques, spare cash to go to the countryside and stay in quaint bed and breakfasts, to be tourists for once. Late at night, I taught myself to type with excerpts from classics like Franz Kafka's *Metamorphosis* or J. M. Barrie's *Peter Pan*. I was certain learning a new skill would transform me. At 11 PM, I cried as I typed, and if the repetition didn't calm me, if it didn't numb my churning thoughts, I cried myself to sleep. Through the bedroom door, I could hear Stella sigh heavily, as she lay curled in her dog bed, like she too was falling apart, waiting for her best friend to return.

It didn't occur to me to get professional help. This time, my breakdown was the catalyst for change; Rick accepted a job in Calgary working for his cousin's electric company, and I enrolled in an online office administration course.

Before we left the island, Esther gifted me a painting of arbutus trees with a glimmer of the ocean between the orange-tinged branches, reminding me of the art project I had wanted to start but never did.

"For your new life," she said.

BAKED OYSTERS JAPANESE-STYLE

One of our favourite things to do is to collect food for free. Gabriola's Brickyard Beach is the best place to collect big fat oysters at low tide. We were first introduced to this recipe at the Japanese restaurant Shabusen in Vancouver. It is a warm and cozy little restaurant with small grills set in the tables to grill your own food. On their menu, these baked oysters, called Oysters Motoyaki, are served hot and bubbling. They are perfect with a cold beer. For a few years, it became our special Christmas outing when we were visiting relatives. In restaurants these are often served on the half shell, but at home, when this is not always possible, we cut the oysters in pieces to fit into little white ramekins. If you collect your own oysters, it is important to return the shells back to the beach, so the baby oysters (spats) can attach and grow on the old shells. You will need 6 ramekins (125-mL) for this recipe.

Feeds 6 as an appetizer

1 cup Japanese Kewpie mayo

1½ tsp miso paste (preferably Mugi)

6–8 fresh large oysters, shelled, or an 8 oz (225-g) package of fresh shucked oysters

½ cup diced white onion

½ cup diced white mushrooms

½ cup chopped green onions

Cayenne pepper or Tabasco sauce

6 tablespoons Panko breadcrumbs

Preheat oven to 400°F. In a small bowl, mix together Kewpie mayo and miso paste. Cut up oysters into bite-sized pieces. Add a teaspoon of mayo/miso mixture on the bottom of each ramekin.

Next add 1 Tbsp of chopped onion and mushrooms to each ramekin. Place bite-sized oyster pieces on top of the vegetables, distributing evenly between the ramekins. Mix the green onions into the remaining miso/mayo mixture, and add 1 Tbsp of the sauce on top of the oysters. Add a sprinkle of cayenne pepper or a dash of Tabasco into each serving. Add 1 Tbsp panko crumbs to each ramekin or enough to cover, pressing firmly so that all ingredients are underneath the breadcrumbs.

Place ramekins on a baking dish and into the preheated oven on the bottom rack and bake for 12 minutes. Broil on high for 2–3 more minutes or until browned. Watch carefully so you don't burn the breadcrumbs.

Note: it is important to use Kewpie Japanese mayo as it is richer and tangier than North American–style mayo.

DORIS DAY AND
A CUP OF LEMON TEA

E MOVED from Gabriola to Calgary with Chloe. Nineteen-year-old Hailey had returned from a year-long trip to Australia. She thought that living in Alberta was beneath her island-girl soul, so she stayed on Gabriola and worked at Mad Rona's Coffee Bar. The transition to city life was difficult for all three of us. We found a townhouse for $1,800 a month through an old friend on Facebook. I needed to find work quickly and sent resumes out in a flurry. I had one interview at which they said they just wanted to meet me because my resume was so odd.

"We've never met a soapmaker."

As far as I could tell, the job involved sniffing urine to make sure work crews were drug and alcohol free. It was well-paid, and their services were in demand. I didn't get a call back.

The next job I found was caring for Pat, the aging mother of a woman named Holly who lived in the same house with her wife and her father, Bruce. As far as I could tell, Holly's main source of income was creating haunted houses where people paid to be scared out of their minds. I kept Pat company so that Bruce could rest in the other room. He had met

Pat as a boarder in her house in Edmonton. They ran away together and that was that; they stayed in love and raised a family. Caring for Pat was meant to be a filler job while I found something more permanent.

While scrolling through an online job board, I noticed that Mountainside Career College was hiring.

I arrived for the interview frozen from the bus ride because I was too afraid to drive on Calgary's icy roads. I sat in the small waiting room, stomping my feet to get the blood back into my toes. Behind the desk was one of the director's sons, a very friendly young Pakistani man. He was chubby-faced with glasses, fast-talking, and smiley. The only other person in the waiting room was a solemn woman in a sari, staring off into space. I later learned she was the wife of the director, Mr. Sayyid, who would be interviewing me. She was checking me out. I was nervous in the interview and shuffled my feet.

I watched as Mr. Sayyid ate slices of an apple with slender fingers. I didn't impress him. I only got the job on a Friday after their first candidate quit right away. (I should have taken this hint.) I was to start on Monday. The job was full time—fifteen dollars an hour, working from 8 AM to 4 PM, five days a week.

I would soon realize my computer skills were barely passable, and I could not for the life of me transfer a call. I practised with Vlad, the HR manager who had hired me. He was my main ally in the office. He would help me practise transferring calls, but no matter how many times we went through the drills, it eluded me. My main job was to answer phones, so this was a big problem. (Before long, Vlad had quit in a huff, for a reason I couldn't decipher. I missed him.)

When someone would appear in the waiting room and say, "Could you tell Mr. Sayyid that x is here?" I would respond, "I'm sorry, could you repeat that?" Eventually, I asked everyone to write down their names on a piece of paper.

Students from Africa had names twenty letters long, like Mr. Ibeamaka Onwuatuegwu, which took me a long time to learn how to spell and pronounce. I was grateful when there was a student from China with the last name Li. These students were paying $18,000 dollars a year to become medical office administrators for a wage similar to mine, though I had no real credentials. They were immigrating to Canada on student visas.

My job also involved dodging creditors who called hourly. I got good at being short with people. Whenever Mr. Sayyid came out of his office, I said, "x called regarding monies owed." I got phone calls from the marketing department of various newspapers and often the landlord, Tom. He eventually gave up and instead sat in the waiting room until Mr. Sayyid had no choice but to invite him into his office. It seemed odd to owe money to so many people at once. I grew nervous Mr. Sayyid wouldn't pay *me*, so I kept careful track of my hours.

The college's teachers were two women greatly overqualified for their jobs. Dr. Zahara was from India and got twenty dollars an hour for four hours a day to teach her students about medical office administration. No benefits. Nimisha was from India as well and was always running late, due to her little girl being in child care. I was the only one called into Mr. Sayyid's office to be reprimanded for accepting a large delivery of computers without counting them.

I was not used to being yelled at, so I wept all the way home, driving the long way, down Shaganappi instead of the terrifying racetrack-like speed limit of the Deerfoot Trail. Along the side of the road were signs that read: BEWARE OF FROST HEAVES AHEAD. I had no idea what that meant, but it sounded dangerous. I consoled myself on the drive home by eating Ferrero Rocher chocolates given to me by Dr. Zahara for Christmas.

I got home twenty minutes later. I had been used to island driving. Speeding meant reaching fifty kilometres an hour in barely any traffic, slowing down for a deer and its fawns grazing in the ditches at twilight, so the fast traffic and heavy snowfall of Calgary was panic inducing. I had to breathe deeply and pinch myself to avoid passing out, but I was determined to make it. I so wanted this change for our family.

It was my job was to put up the office Christmas tree. I was Canadian after all, and I knew about all these things. I was also to put on a party for the students and staff, complete with party games that required you to relay Hershey's kisses while wearing large unwieldy mittens. This turned out to be a great hit. I bought sushi for the potluck, which Mrs. Sayyid seemed eager to try.

Everyone else brought samosas, as usual. I knew how to make samosas from scratch (from my *Moosewood Cookbook* days), which surprised them.

IN THE back room were a few beds set up as a mock hospital room with an old dummy waiting to be turned and washed by students studying to be nurse's aides. Sometimes Mrs. Sayyid took a nap back there, scaring me when I noticed the sheets move, or when I heard snoring. The rest of the time she sat and read a tiny book with gold indecipherable writing. She wore long flowing pants and a scarf around her neck, her hair dyed orange. She made endless cups of tea served in Styrofoam cups mixed with tiny tins of condensed milk. I was the odd one out who brought my own mug. My background in environmental studies makes it impossible for me to use Styrofoam. I tried not to judge, but I couldn't help myself.

Mrs. Sayyid came into work with her husband every day. It was really a family affair. Mr. Sayyid's son Chavdar had gone to school in Victoria, so I was taking his place at the reception desk. Chavdar was about to get married and was going to Pakistan to get his wife.

Mrs. Sayyid occasionally tried to talk to me in English, saying gleefully one day, "Happy anniversary!" I didn't have the heart to tell her I wasn't married. Rick had emailed my work account that morning to make up. We had had a fight the night before. Mr. Sayyid and his wife must have read his words of love and thought it was our anniversary.

Rick was pushing to go back to BC to work as a diver. The night before I had yelled at him from the top of the stairs. "You can't leave us in Calgary!"

Rick had walked out the front door, said he was done. He told me he would spend the night in a hotel somewhere. I ran after him through the snowdrifts, my ugly blue bathrobe flapping open. I didn't care if the neighbours saw.

"Don't leave!" I cried in desperation. It was like the night of the killer lasagna all over again, but this time it was Rick who was pushing for change. Some days he didn't want to get out of bed.

On my last day at Mountainside College, I had the Ministry of Justice on the line. I had taken down the phone number before I transferred the call, in case I accidentally disconnected the caller, which I did. When I told Mr. Sayyid who it was, and that I had cut off the call, he just looked at me, pursed his lips, and walked away with a pained look on his face, stiff-legged like a broken soldier. I was sure he was glad to see me go.

On my last day, the Sayyid family wished me well, kindly saying, "Good luck, Inshallah." *God willing, as Allah wills it.*

SHORTLY AFTER my father Frank moved from Edmonton to Nanaimo, we made the big decision to relocate to Calgary. I was beside myself with guilt at the timing as my father had only just moved from Edmonton to be closer to us. Tanya was now living in Vancouver, and he had tried living in her base- ment suite, which had not worked out. After Frank moved to Nanaimo, Tanya came over on the ferry for a day trip with her kids; she wanted to smooth over their bad parting. We all went bowling at Splitzville. That's where we told everyone the news. We asked Frank to consider moving back to Alberta with us. He hurried outside to smoke a cigarette. When he returned in a cloud of smoke, I nudged Rick with my elbow to remind my father that all of us were on board with the invite. Rick tried to again to get him to consider moving.

Frank was adamant that he would not be joining us, and added with a sneer, "You know, the women in Calgary are all thin."

I knew his comment was meant to be a dig about my weight, and that I should feel angry. The smell of the greasy pizza slabs wilting under the heat lamp made my stomach turn. I felt like I was abandoning a baby on the side of a busy highway. But I was desperate to improve my own family's life, so we moved, leaving Frank behind.

AFTER I got the news that my father was in the hospital, I packed up to return to Nanaimo to see what I could do to help.

Frank was still in his soiled hospital pajamas, despite being discharged five days previously. He had been found uncon- scious by the security guard in the bathroom of the only casino in town. I had known that his heart was bad, and that he had had a cancer scare in the past year, but he never talked about it, and I hadn't bothered to ask

When my father was in the hospital, I had surprised myself and called him in his room in Acute Care and said, my voice cracking, "I love you, Dad."

Our relationship had been turbulent, but I still meant it. Though he hadn't called Tanya or me when our mother died, and he didn't come to the funeral. I later discovered he gave my baba money while she was looking after us.

My friend Esther said, "You don't owe him anything."

I knew this, but I still cared.

I flew in from Calgary on Esther and Eric's air miles and took a taxi to his apartment. In the hall outside my father's apartment door, my backpack listing, I met a young girl holding a plastic basket of laundry coming out of the opposite apartment. I told her I was just visiting.

I heard a young man from inside her apartment say, "Want a punch in the mouth, you ungrateful bitch?" I saw a mattress in the middle of the living room floor. When she closed the door, I heard one of them say, "Who was it?" and another answered, "Your mother!" I heard their laughter and was ashamed that I looked so matronly.

This was where my father chose to spend the final years of his life, although Rick and I had found safer and cheaper options for him in Nanaimo—places with working elevators close to the Nanaimo Regional General Hospital. I had even called a community health nurse for advice. How could I get him into a facility? What were the costs? How long was the wait list? She had told me *he* had to start the process, but he never did.

Inside the three-storey walk-up, I nearly slipped on the blackened linoleum floors. There was an inch of slime on the dishes in the sink. I picked up the mountain of greasy paper takeout bags and empty plastic 7-Eleven cups with remnants of dark liquid bobbing with bloated cigarette butts, shovelled them into an enormous orange plastic trash bag, and hauled them to the dumpster out back. I borrowed his car to pick up cleaning supplies because clearly he had none. His housekeeping skills were on par with those on display in his Edmonton apartment ten years ago. That time I had visited after his heart surgery.

That apartment had resembled a crack den. Chloe had been six and too young to leave with a friend while Rick was away, so I'd brought her with me. I remembered that I washed the toilet before I let her use it, and that I had to give her an allergy pill every day to survive the week-long stay. Each morning I made her play on the balcony with her pink plastic horses while I scrubbed my way through years of orange nicotine stains on the walls. Meanwhile, he would lay on his couch and watch the news from morning to night.

For a breath of fresh September air, Chloe and I had walked through the cool downtown streets to Starbucks for a vanilla latte and a dairy-free brownie. I would bring my father a coffee he'd sip for the rest of the day. I'd do an afternoon cleaning shift, followed by another field trip to the park, and so it went. When he was feeling better, he invited me to come to his AA meeting, but I declined. As a child, I had been dragged to these smokey gatherings, and I didn't want a repeat of them now that I had a choice.

GROWING UP, I remembered the sound of Frank's fists banging on our door late at night, hollering, waking up the neighbours: "Ella! Ella!" He was jealous of Mom's new boyfriend, Clancy. One time Frank broke the glass window in the door and started to cry, an ugly sound for a child to hear that shocked me more than anything. I knew I should be grateful that he quit drinking (off and on), but it had no real impact on my life once he moved out except to put him even more on edge.

As part of the divorce agreement, Tanya and I had to stay with him every weekend. He drove us to and from dance lessons, shaking his fist at cars. "Come on, ya farmer!" We used to sit trapped in his car with the windows rolled up in winter, while he chain-smoked Player's Lights. At restaurants he was cranky with the waitresses, unless, of course, they were attractive. Then he would smile and give them big tips. My father ogled young women with my six-year-old sister at his side because "She was a chick magnet." Sometimes he would pick me up with his stripper girlfriend Sunshine in the front seat of the car. It turned my stomach.

He took us bowling and for Chinese takeout. Tanya and I slept on his scratchy living room couch. We fell asleep at 2 AM to movies about stylish female vampires that gave me nightmares. I would lay awake, wrapping my long hair protectively around my vulnerable neck.

He was an only child coddled by his mother, Little Baba. "She still wiped my ass when I was six years old!" he would say, furious. His father, William Fedoruk, would go on week-long benders, stealing money from the till in their store, Ideal Produce. He died of a stroke when I was thirteen. He had beaten Little Baba, a detail I only learned many years later. This family life may have explained why my father became a broken shell of a man, but it was little consolation to me.

IT WAS years later, when I snapped on the latex-free rubber gloves and began to work away at the orange shit stains that caked the toilet bowl. I pressed my nose against the window screen to get a breath of fresh air.

"You really knew how to pick 'em, Mom," I whispered.

On this visit, Frank was unshaven with only mustard and an old margarine container in his faded orange refrigerator. He had a cheap one-cup coffee maker and some dried cream packets strewn across the stained counter. He still had the hand-painted fish plates I gave him for Christmas over twenty years ago. The saggy single bed in his bedroom was the third-hand bed Hailey and I had brought over one night, when I found out he had been sleeping on the floor. We hauled up the old mattress up three flights of stairs ourselves. He turned on his cheap electric radio to a scratchy station and began to shuffle a little dance on his kitchen floor. He still didn't own a couch.

When my father first moved to Nanaimo, we went on an outing to The Brick. When it became clear that he had no intention of spending more than a few hundred dollars on all his home furnishings, and there was no way I could talk him into new furniture, we had bought him an old brown Value Village fabric chair. The father of a boy at Chloe's school carried the heavy chair up the three flights of stairs, looked around the dismal apartment, and said, "Does he live here alone?"

Once again, I felt ashamed.

THE NEXT day, Frank's home care nurse, Helen, dropped by. She had disheveled blonde hair and was fairly attractive. *This would please him,* I thought. My father couldn't stand women who were ugly or fat, although this might have been an example of the pot calling the kettle black. Helen came up the stairs one at a time, sideways like a crab.

"Bad legs," she said in what I guessed was an Irish accent.

She told me that my father had been assessed in the hospital and had been deemed well enough to live on his own, although he did have "some loss." *Some loss*? Did she know he wanted to go out in public in his brown-stained saggy hospital pajamas?

When Rick called later, I surmised, "They probably just wanted to get rid of him."

In a perfect world, I wished he had agreed to live with us in Calgary. He would have been the Norman Rockwell–like senior who sat in an overstuffed chair by the fire while we binge-watched episodes of *Modern Family* over popcorn. During the Christmas holidays, he would have chuckled quietly at his grandkids' antics, but the truth is, my children barely knew him.

BEFORE I left to return to Calgary, I stocked his cupboards with a loaf of bread, a few cans of soup, and two plastic packets of ham.

A month after that visit, he was found dead in his bathroom in Nanaimo. The RCMP broke down his door when his landlord hadn't received his rent. I am haunted by the memory of our last goodbye, what I said as I heaved him out of his filthy reclining chair, certain that this would be our final hug, trying not to look at the shit stains on the towel he'd folded beneath him.

I can hardly bear to remember the way I had pulled him in close, knowing he hadn't washed for over a week. I will never forget his long brown fingers and the strange softness of his hands.

INUNDATING THE library monthly with resumes had finally paid off. I got a job with the Calgary Public Library. I was hired as a part-time shelver at the Crowfoot branch, a stone's throw from Bruce and Pat's house, where I had my first home care job. Shelving books wasn't a high paying position, but I adored that I could be near books. I loved knowing where each book belonged on the shelves. If a kid stopped by to ask where a certain copy of Geronimo Stilton was, I knew exactly where to locate it, like my body was leading me to it and not the Dewy Decimal system.

Later, I was thrilled when I was promoted to a better position. I adored planning story time, couldn't believe that I now got paid to sing songs to kids. I felt like a queen at the wheel of the company car driving to an outreach in schools or community halls, where I would set up a table and talk up books and our free services. Sometimes I read to a roomful of Cub Scouts or drove along in the book truck to set up at the Sky Train and talked about literature with anyone willing to brave sub-zero temperatures. As I pulled random books from the shelves and read snippets aloud, we laughed and stamped our feet to stay warm. I had a Chinese co-worker who taught me how to say, "My name is Margot" and "library" in Mandarin.

My neighbourhood at home was equally diverse. I thought of this while walking to the garbage unit, suddenly aware of my slouchy pants hastily tucked into muddy rubber boots, my hair windblown and unwashed. I hoped my neighbours weren't peering through the curtains.

When I first saw the Iranian family of six move into the townhouse next door—including a woman covered head to toe in black—I became instantly self-conscious of my pajama bottoms and plaid jacket thrown over my tattered tank top. This was my usual attire for daily errands, from walking the dog to juggling the recycling.

On the rare days I saw my neighbour outside, I couldn't help but note the contrast in our attire and was mesmerized by her long black skirt sweeping the driveway as she moved. Her hair was always covered, so I only saw her face. I didn't know the appropriate name for her clothing in her language, but I had seen many Muslim women wear these robes in the city. They made me think of nuns and period costumes. Perhaps the extra time it took her to cover up kept her from outdoor chores, as she often set the garbage bags just outside her front door, rather than make the trip to our shared garbage unit only steps away.

One day when I walked by my neighbour's small back deck parallel to ours, she invited me in for a visit. She told me her name is Ayesha. I was grateful for her company, as I had found city living to be isolating. When I told Ayesha that I had a cold, she offered to make me a special lemon drink. Inside the privacy of her home, I was surprised to see that she was wearing yoga pants and a clean, white long-sleeved blouse. She had bare feet. Her black headscarf had slipped down so I could see the part in her hair.

As I sat on one of her sofas, I couldn't help but compare our rental units. Their house was an exact replica of ours but in reverse. I admired a painting of trees on the wall and saw that their furniture was colourful but well worn. I glanced at the carpet and my feet, and noticed that Stella's white dog hairs had stuck to my black socks. I uncrossed my legs and tucked my feet under the couch.

Ayesha boiled water, opened and closed cupboards. She answered her cell phone and began to talk in a low voice, in a language I presumed to be Persian. She handed me a delicate saucer supporting a Chinese teacup of hot liquid. As she spoke, she cradled the phone between her shoulder and ear, dragging a small table in front of my knees. I wanted to help her, but the full teacup in my hands rendered me powerless. The table was decorated with an ornate gold cloth with tassels. As she pulled on it, the back legs got stuck. They began to roll up the end of the carpet, so she tamped the table legs down with her foot.

I noticed that her hands were disproportionately large, compared to her fine facial features, and I wondered if this was from years of manual housework. I was reminded of my Ukrainian grandmother (Little Baba) who hand-scrubbed all her clothes on a little washboard with a bar of Ivory soap. She hung them to dry outside her house in the north end of Winnipeg. Every winter she showed me her cracked fingers—"chilblains," she called them.

When Ayesha finally settled onto the sofa across from me, I tried to sneak another look under her black headscarf. I was surprised to see she had dyed blonde hair in a braid that ran along her neck. She played with her scarf constantly, adjusting and pulling it back into place. In the '80s, I fidgeted the same way, hiking up my nylons when the crotch slid to my knees. Now I wear only long pants and short black ankle socks, advice I picked up from *Canadian Living* magazine: "Simplify your life! Always buy the same-coloured socks to eliminate having to sort them."

I TOOK a sip of the hot drink carefully, so as not to burn my tongue. I was expecting an exotic lemon drink, perhaps an ancient family recipe handed down from generations of women in the old country. To my surprise, she served me NeoCitran.

She told me it was her husband, Yoosuf, who had called. "He is scared," she said. "He is having a medical problem." She paused, struggling to find the English word for sinuses. "He has had an operation already but may need another one."

I thought of Rick's power tool accident and the subsequent emergency surgery on his hand.

I nodded in understanding.

Ayesha's oldest son, Amir, went to the same high school as Chloe, a forty-minute bus ride into the centre of the city. We talked about their troubles adjusting and making friends there.

She said, "Why aren't my children happy in Canada where it is so easy? There is no war. There is electricity." She told me her husband didn't like to talk so she called her cousin all the time instead.

We complained about the condo management, wishing we had a garden to work in instead of an endless green lawn watered every morning and pumped with chemical weed killers every spring. Ayesha told me their last home, northeast of the city, was noisy with traffic. She could smell people smoking drugs through the screens in her windows. Having only lived in this part of Calgary, I just nodded and smiled.

Rick and I were lucky to be living in the good part of the city, but the rent was $1,800. We took on a boarder, a young woman named Sarah from Toronto, who answered our ad on Kijiji. She shared a tiny bathroom with Chloe, down the echoing hall from out master bedroom. She liked to start her laundry at 10 PM, the sound of heavy zippers rattling in the dryer, keeping me up for hours. Sometimes she wouldn't leave her room for days. Once when I had finally found the courage to knock on her door, I called out her name, and when there was no answer, I opened the door to her room. Sarah had gone away for a few days, left her car in the driveway, hadn't let me know of her plans. I was certain that she was dead.

I could tell Ayesha only understood half of what I said. She also kept repeating the word *Inshallah,* a term I had heard many times in Calgary. I believe it means, "It is all up to God."

I was nervous she would discover that I am a godless person and wouldn't think highly of me when she saw me drag Stella around the block every day. Usually, I was picking up after her with the pink plastic snow shovel we kept propped against our wooden deck solely for this purpose. How slovenly I must have seemed to her.

I longed to tell her of my complicated Jewish heritage but I didn't. I only associate it with my childhood and no longer think of myself as Jewish. When I moved out west to raise a family, this part of myself disappeared. I recite a few lines of a Hebrew prayer on special occasions as kind of a party trick: "*Barukh ata Adonai, Eloheinu, melekh ha'olam.*" My zayda sung those words over our holiday meals as a prayer of thankfulness. Rick and I have deliberately raised our children in a home without any religious practices.

I got up and thanked my host for the drink, anxious to get the dog walked before going to work.

We stood at the door, smiling and nodding, and agreed that life is hard.

Ayesha said, "What can you do? *Inshallah*."

"Yes, what can you do?" I replied, protesting as she pressed the opened cardboard box of NeoCitran into my hands as I left.

When Chloe got home from running practice, I wanted her to have a hot meal, so I made chili. I would be at work at the library until 9 PM that evening, so I wouldn't see her unless I got up at 7 AM the next day before she would catch the bus to school. I wondered what it would be like to have only one job; my messy soap business in the basement made two, landlady to the boarder made three, just to make ends meet. *Would I feel happier? Less rushed? More fulfilled?* I thought how hard it must be for Ayesha's husband to support their family of six on one salary, and I wondered how he did it. Sometimes I heard them quarrelling through the thin walls that separated our townhomes, their voices rising. Rick and I fight quietly, simmering with long-held resentments. We would be embarrassed to let our neighbours hear us at our worst.

WE DECIDED to move back to BC. I didn't want to admit defeat, but we had already accumulated $40,000 in debt. I had hoped I would be able to climb the ladder at the library, make enough to sell our home on Gabriola, buy a fixer-upper in Bowness, a cheaper neighbourhood in West Calgary. I was disappointed to leave my job. I knew we weren't making a go of it here, financially, or as a family. Chloe missed her friends. Rick's commute was too far. Because of his plane tickets, our credit card bills were racking up. I made an appointment with a phone therapist and wept into the phone. I tried to explain how I really wanted it to work out, tried to explain my desperation about our long-distance marriage. The therapist recommended we call each other daily when Rick was away diving to keep up a close connection. I hung up, feeling a sense of frustration.

The day before we left, Ayesha's two oldest sons, Amir and Muhammad, helped us move our heavy furniture into the moving van. They handed me a box of Purdys chocolates. I dropped by to give Ayesha a bar of my homemade soap and thanked her before we left the city for good.

I remembered the song "Que Sera, Sera (Whatever Will Be, Will Be)," performed by Doris Day, that my mother used to sing in her Volkswagen Rabbit as she drove my younger sister and me to swimming lessons. She sang constantly, despite my father choosing his addictions over her. I don't think my mother ever forgave him. Singing is a habit I inherited from her. I may not believe in a god, but I truly believe whatever will be, will be.

Inshallah.

14

SHADE OF
TOWERING CEDARS

I WAS WALKING a trail in Sandwell Provincial Park with Chloe, who has lived on Gabriola Island for most of her eighteen years. We were headed to find an ancient Snunéymuxw cave burial site near the cliffs. I used to carry her on my back down this same trail when my legs were young and strong. Her eyes were wide, taking in the scenery. On this day, she reached out her hand to help me up the incline.

We were surrounded by green so dark that it soaked up the sun and the moist air had condensed to a damp layer on my skin. In the shadows, we saw what looked like hip bones, burnished with age. At the bottom of the trail, we passed ancient middens, remnants of shellfish feasts.

For nearly two decades, my own family and I have walked this eight hundred–metre trail—bath towels carelessly slung over our shoulders, our fat dog Stella poking along behind. Passing the moss-covered trunks of the bigleaf maples, Rick often remarked, "Look at those burls. I could make something great with those." At home we have Mason jars filled with beach glass worn smooth, reminders of meals on damp sandy towels in the heat of summer.

If you lie in the sand and position your body facing the marsh, you can imagine a time when the Snunéymuxw canoed here to harvest clams. This was before the Spanish arrived, bringing smallpox with them. Though the Snunéymuxw couldn't know their fate, they likely found solace on this stretch of sandy beach, mothers and fathers pulling their children in close, breathing in the cool ocean air, watching a kingfisher dip its head into the sea.

When the tide is low, we often take the shortcut back along the crescent-shaped shore, leaving footprints in the cold hard sand, past pitted sandstone boulders, barnacles, and purple starfish clinging to their sides. In the shade of towering cedars, two rock carvings—petroglyphs known to locals—stand guard. One carving is of a stick figure with an arrow, possibly inauthentic, and the other is a faded round "face" looking up at the sky.

Gabriola Island is also known as Petroglyph Island, with over seventy rock carvings scattered across the island. The best spot to view them is behind the United Church off South Road, especially if wet weather has darkened the petroglyphs' grooves.

On rainy days when our kids were young, Rick and I would watch as Hailey and Chloe ran ahead of us; more recently, I have brought my walking stick to maneuver the trails, despite arthritic knees. Sometimes Stella would perk up from her week-long nap to join me. Although her gait was slowing with age, she rallied to sniff the salal-lined path and ancient ferns.

I stopped to read the large white sign at the trailhead, erected by BC Parks that explains it is difficult to date rock carvings that could be one hundred to three thousand years old. There are many petroglyphs in the clearing at the end of the path, including one that reminds me of the plumed head of the local belted kingfisher. I was impressed by its smooth curvy lines. Petroglyphs were made with handmade tools called hammerstones that pecked the lines into the rock. I fought the urge to scrape back moss on flat surfaces to check for more lines underneath.

Gabriola's forests, flat bedrock, and honeycombed sandstone along the fifteen-kilometre length of the island were ideal for capturing the local flora and fauna. Other carvings are otherworldly and intentionally unrealistic. The most impressive is a sea serpent or a "lightning snake" that resembles the Indigenous haietlik, a mythical creature with razor-like teeth ideal for the whale hunt.

Explorers noticed the haietlik images painted onto the sides of local canoes. I also recognized salmon similar to those in Jack Point and Bigg's Petroglyph Park in Nanaimo. With the decline of the Snunéymuxw population, due to outbreaks of disease, the meaning of the carvings has largely been lost, but some stories remain and have been recorded and told to non-Indigenous audiences.

A traditional story about the Jack Point petroglyphs explains that a dog salmon took the form of man to steal the chief's daughter to be his wife and return with her to the sea. The dog salmon and his wife swam upriver leaping out of the water together. The chief went north to search for his daughter and was told she would return once a year to Nanaimo but could not go home with him. During the yearly salmon run, only the chief and his descendants in their village were permitted to touch the salmon, roast it, and eat it whole. It could not be cut up for drying or smoking until the shaman performed a ceremony in front of the salmon petroglyphs. He painted a male and female dog salmon with red ochre sprinkled with eagle down, shook his rattle, and sang over the fish as everyone joined in.

Now, once a year on the south end of Gabriola, islanders join together for a giant salmon barbecue at the community hall. We spread blankets on the grass and eat slabs of salmon with potato salad and a wedge of watermelon. Local musicians play on stage while face-painted children chase each other and dance barefoot on the grass. Ice cream, beer, and fish sales raise money for the hall and the playground, a place where we once found a nest of baby garter snakes writhing in the sun.

NOW THAT our daughters have grown up and left home, Rick and I trek the easier sandstone shore of the beach where I held my father's memorial four years ago, releasing his ashes into the sea that hot August day. Rick had been away working and was unable to return in time, so my sister Tanya and I had organized the events. We set out blankets beneath the spreading branches of a maple tree to eat stuffed figs and chicken wraps.

Both Hailey and Chloe had taken the day off from their jobs at local restaurants and my sister Tanya and her two children, Emily and Zach, took the ferry from their home in Vancouver. Zach found a flat piece of driftwood to balance the fancy cardboard box containing my father's ashes. Frank was born in Winnipeg, yet he asked to have his remains released near the shore where he took his grandchildren to catch fish in rocky tidepools. We played drumming music from a CD player while Tanya placed colourful dahlias in the water. I read from a crumpled piece of paper. It took only minutes for the water to overturn the piece of wood and lap my father's ashes out to sea.

I have learned that young men on spirit quests would lie prone on the petroglyphs to receive the power of these symbols. This landscape echoes their stories, the stories of the Snunéymuxw, but also my father's story, and all those who once walked these trails.

When Rick and I stop to rest on the wooden bench overlooking the ocean, I imagine the day we will walk here with our grandchildren so they can play below on the rocks. The smooth head of a seal dips under the silver-grey water, and I think of all those lost to us.

In the heat of summer, in the wind or pelting rain, I am compelled to visit these paths lined with Garry oaks and echoing with the prehistoric voices of sea lions from across the strait. I stand here, watching in the mist for canoes, for a couple of leaping salmon, for my father, and I listen for their stories.

I KNELT on the damp grass, hands searching for the last bit of warmth from Stella's slumping head.

Her lungs were expelling slow deep breaths, weary from this heavy life. We wept as we left her body splayed on the cool green grass, sun slanting over the clinic roof. The vet had just administered her last needle. He waited by her side and told me that it was okay to go. I stumbled into the car and nodded at Rick to drive away.

At home, we drank vodka in the afternoon, sat in the garden, pulled weeds from between rows of garlic, fed the neighbour kids kale flowers through the fence. We sat staring into the foliage, eyes watering from the dying light. Inside, we poured more vodka, trying to hold back tears, and listened to a playlist while we made salmon and prawns, and wept to Neil Young's soulful voice as he sang "Harvest Moon." Gone were the beach days when Stella would bound into the sea chasing rocks, her muzzle plunging into salt water. Before she died, she had been an old blind dog with rotting teeth who once jumped off a dock into the cold ocean—even though she was afraid of the water—because she couldn't bear to be left behind.

Later, we held each other, exhausted, empty, hearing only silence. No more long dog walks, tripping over roots, dragging around black plastic bags.

"It's just us again," Rick said with a tremor in his throat.

"That's not so bad, is it?" I replied, unsure.

STANDING UNDER the bright white lights of London Drugs, I leaned against the smudged glass counter of the cosmetics department, waiting to buy a marriage license. An elfish woman, ahead of me in line, attempted to engage me in conversation about glittery press-on nails. I knew she must be high; her eyes were wild, and she moved her limbs in odd jerks. I hoped this wasn't a bad sign.

I shifted my weight from one leg to the other while waiting for Bruce, the manager, who must log in to the registry. I recognized him from the day before, his large stomach straining against a cheap blue shirt and a Christmas tie with a reindeer on it. I am fifty-three years old, and I have never been married.

Rick and I had made an attempt to get married a few years ago on my favourite beach at Sandwell Provincial Park. I had booked the commissioner and planned the vows, but Rick's work schedule changed, and he was unable to make the date. I surprised myself and wept. Rick almost always makes it home for December 24, so I tried again. Besides, I wanted to rid myself of the feeling that I could just get up and leave. I believed if we were married, I would no longer have an escape route. When Rick was gone for too long, these thoughts swirled around in my head: *We're not married, I can leave! Start over somewhere else, with somebody else.* I wanted to banish these urges with an official piece of paper.

The skittish, elfin woman was skulking around the counter at London Drugs and combed her hair with a blue plastic brush, perhaps off the shelf, as she listened in on our conversation. Bruce returned, and I was getting impatient. I wanted a Hollywood moment, but instead Bruce was trying to decipher my soon-to-be husband's birth certificate.

"Is his first name Richard?" he asked, as if someone's first name could be Corless. I noticed the ring on Bruce's finger, gold with a diamond. He was married and he looked fairly chipper. I wanted to surprise Hailey and Chloe with a gift that celebrated the love of their parents, but what if this attempt failed, too? Were the gods conspiring against us?

My good friend Wendy is a trained marriage commissioner. She was planning to drop by for an impromptu party on December 24. The girls would tidy the house. Hailey would make a seafood paella with fresh sea urchin that Rick would catch. After twenty-seven years it might really happen. The wedding was my idea; I needed to close the escape hatch, and refuse to hold anything back.

Earlier that morning, I had met with my advisor at the university, had an appointment at the writing centre, and then joined an event protesting violence against women commemorating December 6, the thirtieth anniversary of the Montreal Massacre, with thirteen other women who told their stories or read poems. We cried as we talked about a world where our daughters weren't afraid to speak up, where they would grow up safe, secure, and strong. I bumped into Chloe on her way to class and felt so proud that she was attending university. Her hair was swept up in a bun, and she was dressed for comfort with scuffed Blundstones and a secondhand sweater. I loved that I was keeping a secret from her, normally hard to do.

Back at the drugstore counter, my swollen knees ached with arthritis. *Maybe Rick and I should marry before we are both in wheelchairs as big as vinyl boats manipulated by strong-armed nurses,* I thought. I was nervous about missing the ferry back to Gabriola, but also about so many other things.

"I have a friend named Richard," the elfin woman blurted. When she realized what I was up to, my heart sank.

"Congratulations," she said.

I told Bruce that Winnipeg is in Manitoba, and I also corrected the month of Rick's birth. Bing Crosby's "The Twelve Days of Christmas" with the verse "Seven Swans a-Swimming" was playing over the loudspeaker. I was briefly comforted. I took a deep breath and bravely paid one hundred dollars for the licence and then headed to the sweets aisle for a box of Lindt Crème Brûlées. *Was I stress eating or celebrating?* I was not certain.

I WAITED impatiently for Rick to call when he got back to his motel room. I sat in my corner of the secondhand couch from his brother and realized the only person I wanted to tell about the drama at London Drugs ... was Rick.

"You should come and visit. The Panorama has an ocean view," he told me, trying to lure me in. When I looked up the hotel online, the website stated that it is a storm watchers' paradise. I have not met him at a hotel since the fatal visit to the Vista del Mar when Chloe was a colicky newborn. That sleepless visit turned the tables, but there wasn't much holding me back now.

WE WERE more tender to each other as the wedding approached. At night, we held hands in bed. I was filled with a wild kind of joy and keeping the secret added an extra bit of charm. I was also proud of the fact that it would cost us less than five hundred dollars for the whole shebang, *and* that was including my haircut with highlights and a new pair of pants. Wendy gave us her marriage commissioner services for free and Marin gifted us the simple silver wedding bands that she had made for us.

On the day of the wedding, I had my hair touched up at the hairdresser's. I was surprised my daughters didn't clue in that something was up, as I rarely fussed about my hair. We also never invited people over on Christmas Eve, so I was worried that they might get suspicious. It was normally the four of us lounging in stretchy yoga pants and stained T-shirts as we feasted on gourmet oysters while watching old movies like *White Christmas*.

On the day of the wedding, Chloe helped tidy the house and Hailey prepped for an elaborate vat of paella. Only three friends were in on the secret: Marin because she handcrafted the rings, Wendy because she was performing the ceremony and my friend Kathy, who had forgiven me long ago for my bad behaviour. "We have to be best friends even when we're old," she said as we wept and hugged each other after I had returned from Calgary.

I had to reveal our plans to Kathy because she had to rally her whole extended family to our house on Christmas Eve.

At the party, when I called for everyone's attention, Hailey looked annoyed because her paella was ready to eat and she didn't want to singe the rice. Chloe later told me her first thought was that we were getting a divorce. I laughed and asked her why would we host a party with our good friends and a two-tiered plate crowded with caramel and espresso-flavoured macarons to announce bad news?

Before we said our vows, we played Israel Kamakawi-wo'ole's version of "Somewhere Over the Rainbow." After the ceremony, Rick kept repeating how lucky he was to get married in a T-shirt and his bare feet. I was overcome by emotions, couldn't stop crying, and Rick thought it was that I was so sad to be marrying him. Later, when we went over the handful of photos, I noticed the shabby scene, behind us a scraggly Christmas tree that was yanked from a corner of the backyard, the coloured lights that made its branches sag. I noticed our wall of homemade art, a chaotic version of my mother's art wall from my childhood home.

When I retell the story of our wedding, I love emphasizing the surprise aspect of the event, how Chloe and Hailey never suspected a thing—because maybe I had, in fact, surprised myself at how much I had wanted to marry Rick.

LIKE FISH
TO WATER

AFTER OUR home wedding, Hailey swept up the kitty lit-
ter, packed up her kitten Pinto, and went back to her life
in Victoria just as Chloe took the ferry to her Nanaimo
apartment. The house was silent once more. Rick
and I headed to Campbell River for our "honeymoon" at the
Ramada Inn, an upgrade from his usual motel across town—
pool, hot tub, and breakfast included.

Winter storms blew hard off the coast, but Rick left for the
boat every morning before I awoke and didn't return from
the dive boat, *The Miss Carmen*, until twelve hours later. Two
young men under his watch now do most of the diving: Gra-
ham and Billy are in their twenties. When I first met Billy, I
asked if his girlfriend minded that he worked away from
home so much.

"She doesn't like it," he admitted. "But I love diving. Can't
believe how lucky I am to do it for a living."

When Rick returned each evening, we ordered dinner
from Royal Zayka, Rick's favourite Indian restaurant in town:
spicy beef vindaloo extra hot and butter chicken for me.

After I woke up each morning, I wandered down to the breakfast room at 8 AM to put my low carb diet on hold to indulge in freshly made waffles. Meanwhile, Rick had been up for hours working in the cold and unforgiving elements. The room was filled with families coming to visit grandparents for the Christmas holidays. The TV hanging from the ceiling droned the news, so I headed back to the room.

Later in the day, I bundled up, stuffed my hat down over my ears, and walked the sea wall past the roiling ocean and the logs on the beach. I hobbled on my bad knees to FoggDukkers coffee shop with its uneven floors to sit on stained lawn furniture, littered with crumbs, listening to the wind blow through the cracks in the wall.

Across from me was a young tourist couple sipping coffee and staring into their cell phones. The woman looked up at me and smiled. We recognized each other from the breakfast room at the Ramada.

I looked across at the Vista del Mar, the same concrete building from two decades ago when I was holed up with Chloe as a colicky newborn and Hailey was doing backflips over the furniture. There was no coffee shop back then, no chainsaw sculptures on every corner, but the stretch of slate grey ocean and the matching sky was familiar. On the beach, a grandmother stood on the edge of the water, rain pelting her face as she encouraged her grandson to throw rocks into the ocean. I did the same with Hailey at that age, with Chloe bundled up tight against my chest. You can lead a child to water, and they may take to it like a fish. Perhaps that's what happened the first time Rick saw the sea. My father taught me to skip rocks on the flat surface of a lake when I was ten.

I walked back along the sea wall past a wooden sculpture of a raccoon wearing a red Santa hat. My eyes were watering, and I walked quickly to escape the biting wind. I saw eagles perched on jutting rocks at eye level. My walking sticks whistled as I looked up at the mountains, black and snow covered. How did Rick have the gumption to jump into the dark icy water in the dead of winter, not knowing what is lurking under the surface?

On the way back to the hotel, I noticed that the hot tub was not crowded and decided to take the plunge. The water was only tepid, but the young woman from the coffee shop was in there. I learned that she was Korean. She said her visiting sisters from Korea found Vancouver night life very dull, but she and her husband love exploring the wilderness, hiking on their time off. I agreed, and then excused myself to climb into the cold water of the swimming pool to do laps. Afterward, I joined her in the sauna. It was barely room temperature, so we climbed back into the hot tub.

Her husband was a tall, serious-looking redhead who walked into the pool room, fully dressed. He whispered something in her ear. She explained that he wanted to go for another walk. I secretly hoped that he wasn't a bully, and that they were going back to their room to make love.

ONE EVENING Rick got back early enough to join me in the hot tub, and as we relaxed in the swirling water, gazing at the fading mural of merpeople, Rick reminded me that we had been here before. We had just discovered I was pregnant, and he had said, "I can tell you are going to be a great mother." *How could he tell,* I wondered?

Later, I laundered Rick's wet work clothes in the little laundromat next to the miniature golf course. In the fluorescent-lit building, I met the young couple again. They heated up an enormous noodle bowl for dinner in the battered microwave. They looked embarrassed.

I was envious. They were in the first phase of love, a magical immersion in an unfamiliar world. I pulled Rick's clothes—a snarl of long underwear, black sweatpants, a jumble of socks—out of the dryer and hauled the armload back to our room.

"You're too good to me," he said when I returned. He watched me fold his clothes, hang his jacket on the back of the chair so he could find it easily in the morning dark. He will kiss me on the ear then and say, "Goodbye. I love you." His whiskers will tickle my cheek, and I will smile, turn over, and fall back to sleep.

ON NEW Year's Day I walked alone along the waterfront without a whisper of wind. The whole town was out, smiling. Young families pushed strollers with panting dogs straining on leashes. An elderly couple dressed in matching outdoor gear, faces flushed from power walking, looked at two eagles swooping over the calm ocean. *Everything comes in pairs,* I thought. I tried not to feel sorry for myself.

BACK ON Gabriola, Rick resumed work on the driveway, industriously sawing lumber or power sanding maple cabinets for the kitchen. I poked my head outside the door to see a cloud of dust illuminated by the sun, and I was comforted to know he was in the middle of it. The yard is littered with heaping piles of wet lumber, the carcass of an unfinished wooden kayak he began in the garage in Calgary four years ago. Mosquito larvae grows in the puddles pooling in tarps.

When he came in for lunch, dripping sawdust, he sat down to fried eggs with sliced avocado and a crumble of feta cheese on corn tortillas. He rubbed his back against the handle of the refrigerator like a bear against tree bark.

"This is great," he said as he devoured his eggs. Every meal is Rick's favourite. It is very satisfying to serve someone so appreciative.

After lunch, when I walked to the shed, the new mast he was working on was inconveniently in my path, and my sweater snagged on a corner of it. Rick is a beaver, always building a better deer fence, fixing the deck, bucking firewood. As he sawed, I noticed his arms were pale from being in a jacket all day, but his face was craggy from the west coast wind.

When Rick is called back to work, he drops everything. I got mad when I found the lawnmower rusting in a corner out back, left in the relentless rain. He never got around to building stairs to his shop, so I awkwardly haul myself up when I need to find a hammer in the jumble of tools on his messy shelves.

When he is gone, I crave his smell, a mixture of diesel fuel and salty air caught in his thick fading orange curls. Old ladies used to stop him on the street to rustle his natural curls when he was young. It embarrassed him, so now if he is sitting in his recliner watching TV, I place a finger on the top of his head where a tiny bald spot is forming.

"What are you doing? I am not going bald!" he protests.

I think like Samson it will kill him to lose his hair. I worry when he can't raise his shoulder to put on his seat belt. Luckily, we are both falling apart at the same time.

"You look the same to me as the day we met," he said after a bottle of homemade Pinot Noir, with my feet wedged under his thighs, stealing the warmth.

At night he wrestles with the bedsheets, thrashes around like a fish in a net. I am afraid to wake him, in case he never gets back to sleep. In the morning, he stands in the shower, water flowing from his long red hair and beading down his broad back. He is wild, and I cannot resist reaching for him because too many times I have reached over to his side of the bed and found nothing but empty sheets, forgetting that he left the day before or even the week before.

There are times when Rick is gone, and my emotions ache at the base of my throat—like the sharp spines of a fish. I wish for a goddess of storms; a benevolent woman listening to the prayers to take mercy on desperate fishwives, who peers down from the clouds with a compassionate face. Like Little Baba's Mary. I imagine she understands the late-night murmuring of women waiting at home for their men. I pray for Rick to be heading home safely down the highway with his dive bag full of damp clothes, pungent with the scent of diesel fuel and sweat. This goddess for fishwives doesn't care that I don't believe in a male god somewhere past the Earth's stratosphere. She doesn't care that I am not a practising Catholic, not entirely Jewish either. She is the saint of desperate fishwives, non-denominational, wise, all-knowing, and a good cook to boot.

RICK WAS normally home in June, but one summer he got a job as a deckhand on a prawn boat.

"I just saw an albino killer whale," Rick said on one of our nightly phone calls. I was sitting on our secondhand couch, wearing Rick's blue flannel pajama bottoms.

"Why don't you come and visit me in Sooke?"

He was staying in a shabby motel with a view of a busy parking lot. I wouldn't be able to sleep when he snores (he is louder when he is exhausted) and would have to stuff orange plugs deep into my ear canals. He wouldn't be able to stay up past 7 PM.

THAT SEPTEMBER, Rick leased a second-hand trailer called *Wildwood* and parked it up in Sayward, a hundred miles from nowhere.

"I can get a Wi-Fi signal if I put my phone in the corner. Can't move it though," Rick explained. "And I bought a chair," he told me proudly.

"Don't get too comfortable."

"What do you mean?"

"I would like you to come home now and then," I said with more anger than I had intended, forgetting to be grateful.

Last week he came home long enough for me to make him zucchini pizza with bacon and a spelt flour crust. We watched *Jeopardy*, hollering out the answers in gentle competition. He left the next morning on the 6:20 ferry. Ice cream and 33 Acres of Sunshine beer were not helping me find peace.

"I'M WAITING for my frozen lasagna to heat up," he told me one night.

I inhaled deeply, remembering my breathing lessons from yoga.

"Well, have a good evening," I choked with a bone-stuck-in-throat feeling. "I love you," I whispered.

"Aww," he said.

I knew he wanted to talk. He knew that I had started therapy. I was instructed to explain to Rick that I love him, but couldn't talk because I didn't want to say things I would regret, such as, "Why the fuck be married to someone you never see?"

Last week a neighbour dropped by to pick up a pound of spot prawns. *I really am a desperate fishwife*. Each morning I drive to the main road to put up a black board that says in smudged chalk: WILD BC SPOT PRAWNS. FRESH FROZEN! BUY LOCAL. We have two deep freezers parked in the corner of the living room underneath a painting of Rick in a dive mask, the regulator stuffed in his mouth.

"Bet you are happy to have the place to yourself," a customer said as they juggled three packages of prawns back to their car.

"No." I said with more anger than I had intended.

I fumed as I washed the dishes. I couldn't help myself. I got testy when people suggested that I would get used to being alone.

At yoga, my friend Marin, who besides being a jeweller, teaches classes on the side. She filled a tiny vase with sunflowers and placed it in the middle of the floor, urging us to practise gratefulness that will spread to other parts of our lives. I was certain she was looking at me.

One night I watched the movie *Three Colours: Blue* with Juliette Binoche, then read a chapter from Gabriel Garcia Marquez's *Love in the Time of Cholera*. The long-married couple fight about a bar of soap and slowly come back together, are led to each other like fish to water.

I PICTURED myself as Ruth Reichl, undercover, a glamorous food critic in a stifling yet realistic- looking wig, here to sample the Sui Mai sweating under the stacked metal tins in the buffet at Moon Garden, one of Nanaimo's long standing all-you-can-eat Chinese restaurants.

Of course, this was all in my head. I was just an average-looking woman out for dinner with my family. I wore scuffed Blundstones, no wig, no makeup. I let Rick choose this venue because it was his birthday.

Rick knows I am no longer a fan of all-you-can-eat buffets. I despise the feeling that I must stuff myself to get my money's worth. This evening, uncharacteristically, and as a special birthday gift, I held my tongue.

Our daughter Chloe, who was twenty when we had this meal, recalled falling asleep years ago in one of the booths as we lingered over a pot of oolong tea, warming our fingers after standing for hours in the lashing wind and rain, the typical weather for coastal winter soccer games. This was our venue of choice after many soccer games with her sister Hailey, who now lives in Victoria and couldn't make this evening's soirée.

It was here at Moon Garden that I first tried sui mai: small, steamed dumplings filled with pork. I once marveled at their delicate texture. But that evening I fond the sui mai tasteless and slick with oil; the brown twists of ginger beef I once loved, were sickly sweet. The decor was the same as from ten years prior, still clean, but many of the booth's faux red leather looked like seagulls had aggressively pecked holes.

I asked Chloe if she remembered how I used to pretend to read their tea leaves. She laughed and says she did. I peered into my tiny handleless cup, and the face of Korean dictator Kim Jong-un appeared. I decided to keep it to myself, not wanting to appear cranky (if only Rick knew how hard I was trying!). Because I knew Rick was drawn to Moon Garden, not for the ominous-looking mussels brought in from New Zealand that he heaped onto his plate, but for the memory of a time when we were the center of our children's world.

This craving for Szechuan food that is kept at a tepid temperature, which caused me to worry about bacterial growth—is like my yearning for the grilled cheese sandwiches of my youth, made with Cheez Whiz and Wonder Bread. The quest is not really for the food but for the sense of being time-travelled back to cherished memories.

The walls of Moon Garden echo with the ghosts of pint-sized soccer players with socks cinched up to their thighs, angelically nodding off as Rick and I finished our squares of Nanaimo bars that tasted like they were came from a box. It didn't matter that the chicken balls were battered to within an inch of their lives. For $19.95 per person, we both knew the food was beside the point.

IT WAS the summer of 2020, and my niece Emily's skin was pale, almost see-through. She has dark hair like her mother, Tanya. Her smile stretched right up into her eyes when the shock of the cold ocean water hit the backs of her knees. We were swimming at Turtle Rock, a popular swimming spot for islanders. She was wearing her new red bikini, which Tanya reminded me must be hand washed and hung to dry, because it was expensive.

Tanya had said Emily was having anxiety issues. I thought of my mother's friend Sonia whose mother who struggled to make it through the day. The weight of losing her whole family to war at seventeen was too much to bear. She wouldn't have been much older than Emily. *What kind of aunt have I been all these years? Too busy? Too immersed in my own issues?* When Emily was young, she would come over to our house with her little brother, and I would play punk rock, and we would dance, her little hands clutching mine, as I bounced her high in the air, feet hovering over the couch cushions. I had done it with Tanya when she was a little girl too, except to "Funky Town."

On this visit, Emily slept in the spare room, pale blue walls lined with Hailey's posters; a Banksy gun-toting panda, a map, three sections of a whale. Hailey had left behind a snarl of twinkle lights and an abandoned clothes hamper with balled-up socks and holey towels. Rick was worried I would be lonesome when he went prawning, so he was relieved that Emily had come to see me. I thought she could use a breather from her own family dynamics, from Tanya. She is a loving mother, but she can be controlling, according to a group of spiritual healers she has consulted. I rolled my eyes, although I secretly hope they will help her find her way to peace.

"I may have PTSD. My brain doesn't work," Tanya said to me.

"I think your brain is working just fine," I replied, reminding her of the good decisions she has made, like buying a rental property on Gabriola after her divorce and the sale of their house in East Vancouver.

When Tanya visits, she sleeps in a tent in the backyard with her dog Comet, not wanting to be a bother. She told me a story about someone she knows who lost weight by taking cider vinegar pills.

"Hmm," I said, pursing my lips, knowing the remark was pointed and intended for me.

When she drove us around the island in her new electric car, and Comet panted and whined between us, I said nothing.

"He's just excited that we are going somewhere fun," she explained.

She left after only two days, saying she couldn't leave her cat and her son Zach's iguana alone too long; besides she had to take on shifts at work. Zach didn't want to leave his friends to come to the island.

EMILY REMAINED for the rest of the week to help me sell soap at the markets. She reminds me of Tanya when she was small, quiet in the shadow of our mother. I can't stop comparing her to my own girls at her age. They were already working full time, Hailey had travelled to Peru. Emily was taking an online chemistry course to get ahead of next year's classes, but she was struggling and missed a quiz.

Tanya said to me on the phone, "I don't care. It was her idea after all."

During Emily's visit, we sat on the rocks by the beach, warming ourselves and talking with my friend Wendy and Rick.

"The last time we came here for a swim, I didn't have water shoes," I told them. "So, Rick took off his old Crocs, worn thin and too large for my feet, so I could wear them while he hobbled barefoot over the sharp rocks. He walked on barnacles for me. That's love."

At the end of the week, I drove Emily to the Departure Bay ferry. She was nervous as we walked into the ferry terminal.

"Let's see if you can figure it out," I said. And she did.

When you have a parent, who is strong and capable, it is easy to forget you can do things for yourself.

As I watched Emily leave, shouldering her large backpack, I remembered Hailey heading off to Peru, using Esther's air miles, taking a ridiculously long route with many exchanges.

I had wished for less adventurous children then, but now I am secretly proud of them. I hope they did not inherit my fear, that they don't let anxieties build up. When I first moved out west in my early twenties, I was terrified when driving that I'd take the wrong lane and be unable to get onto the off-ramp leaving the highway. I would clutch the steering wheel, grit my teeth, with my heart pounding.

After I was sure Emily had safely boarded the big ferry, I headed to Superstore, not wanting to waste the cost of a ferry ride over to Nanaimo. I headed to the pharmacy to buy cider vinegar pills.

On the drive back to the Gabriola ferry, a street person was begging at the busy intersection. I handed him a fiver, and he asked to borrow a pen.

"Keep it," I said. I saw the oncoming traffic and I couldn't stop myself. "Careful," I said.

On the phone later, Tanya said they might come visit in August. She said this hesitantly, like it is hard for her to admit we might need each other.

I have always sought the help of strangers first: a Thai couple down the hall from our apartment in Victoria, who lent me their baby stroller and babysat in a pinch. On Gabriola, Esther, my old boss, now a good friend, picked us up if our cabin was snowed in, and our neighbour Ode dropped by if the power was out, and Kathy took the girls on an annual trip to Parksville to play mini golf to celebrate when school was out.

More recently, when Leigh, a friend in my nightly swim group, didn't contact the office after her home care shift was over, Rick drove me to her tiny pink cabin in the darkening night.

"Oh my God, I forgot to call. I am so sorry I worried everyone!" she said when she opened her door and I explained why I was standing on her porch.

It takes an island.

DESPITE THE fact that he was gone for the past month, Rick was leaving on a fishing holiday for a week to go to Campbell River with his brother Adrian and a fellow diver named Billy. Billy's girlfriend was also not happy about it.

On this trip, Rick would fill our deep freeze with halibut and pink salmon to accompany the whole frozen octopus and the forty-pound bag of grass-fed beef fat I had been meaning to make into tallow for soap-making.

I didn't want to be bitter about Rick the way my mother was about my father. I wanted to see him for who he is. Perhaps I am just like my father who wanted to write poetry in the chicken barn, feathers flying around his head.

That day was hot, so I met Wendy and Leigh at Turtle Rock beach at 6 PM. I live for these summer nights when we can swim in our saggy old suits and sit on the rough rocks speckled with pine sap. I waded in slowly, as is my nature, letting the sun warm my shoulders, and thought about making tuna poke with fresh lime and a handful of cilantro from our garden.

Later that night my friend Marin called and told me that I was lucky to fight with Rick. She lost her husband in a boating accident when her daughter was an infant. I call her when I need someone to remind me of what I already know—that I am surrounded in the best possible way.

"LOOK, 1:11, an angel sign," Tanya said pointing to the numbers on the dashboard. I bit my lip and didn't say a word. She can read my silences, as sisters often can. She launched into a story about Zach witnessing a miracle. I only half listened.

She decided to divorce her husband when he gave her an ultimatum after their retriever died: "Don't get another dog, or that's it for our marriage."

She reckoned she got more love from a dog than from her husband, so that was it. She got a Catahoula cross, which has cost her hundreds a month in dog walkers while she works twelve-hour shifts at the hospital.

I was distracted by Comet's hot breath and whimpering. I wanted to tell her to watch *The Dog Whisperer with Cesar Millan*. She gave Comet a hemp "calming cookie" and was afraid that he was stoned. We both snorted with laughter, and I was reminded of how we used to set out candles and would open a bottle of good red wine, playing Scrabble with our two cats on the bed, steam radiators hissing above the hardwood in the dead of a Winnipeg winter. We would laugh the unbridled laughter of women briefly carefree. Such was life before husbands, children, houses.

Tanya's rental house on Gabriola was occupied by a retired principal and his wife, who paid rent and liked to do repairs around the property, so she rarely had to check on it. When she would come to the island, she wouldn't even accept a spot to stretch out on our secondhand couch. Our family is oddly stoic in this way. She handed me a wad of twenties to help pay for groceries, ice cream, bowls of popcorn.

Emily at sixteen years of age had Tanya's wry sense of humour and kept climbing up on the deck bench to peek at the new baby juncos that have made a nest in a colourful hanging basket. She and her mother were dazzled by the wildlife, the deer grazing along the road, even Tabby cats.

Tanya stopped her car in the middle of the road for every wild thing, and it unnerved me. I would always crank my neck to make sure we were not going to be rear-ended, even though to her these winding roads seemed deserted.

Tanya was always on the hunt for lucky turkey feathers and jumped out and grabbed them from the side of the road, likely crawling with diseases. I said nothing about this or about the signs and the piles of money she gives spiritual healers to help her understand the trauma of her past. I try not to be judgmental.

In fact, the more that I think about it, asking a stranger for advice seems like a good idea. I too have moments when I feel an intense need for help, and I don't know where to find answers. We both worry that we have passed our anxieties to our children.

I love her with fierceness and determination so when she makes phone calls looking for advice, I just try to be supportive. When I moved west, she followed me. When I took a nurse's aide course, she took a nurse's aide course, and it has served her well. I used to say to my sister she was the crazier one, but I realize this is not true. We are both suffering from the shrapnel of our childhood. Now, both of us are searching for answers in every corner.

LATER, AS we waded into the cold ocean water with the sun warming our backs, Tanya admitted, "When Comet dies, I will probably have time to find myself. He is so distracting." She also admitted she only half believes in the spiritual healers, "perhaps it is all a scam."

I was secretly relieved to hear this. I feel protective as her older sister, similar to how she dotes on Emily. She delivered a bowl of washed cherries and a glass of water to her in bed the way I have peeled slippery yellow chunks of mango and handed them to Hailey and Chloe hunched over their laptops.

I remember when we first moved in together in our little basement suite in Winnipeg. If Tanya was mad, she wouldn't talk to me for days. I would follow her, trying to get her to laugh or trick her into answering me. "Do you want your eggs scrambled?" I would ask, hoping for a response, but she was stubborn and not easily fooled.

She also hated how I cooked everything in one pot. During breakfast one morning, Tanya stabbed a chunk of garlic with the tine of her fork and held it up to my face accusingly. "Garlic? Who puts garlic in everything? Ugh!"

At that time, Sonia had given me a job in her family's ticket booth to help me get by. The silence of the snow-muffled booth was broken only by a radio tuned to CBC, a little plug-in heater, and the scratch of my pen as I wrote in my journal. I had just returned for my mother's last days, left my two jobs in Whistler. My friend Corinne's mom gave us gift certificates for groceries. Everyone thought I needed advice, but now I am the one doling it out.

Whenever Tanya called, I recommended a book. "Have you read *The Dance of Anger*? Or what about Tony Robbin's *Awaken the Giant Within*?"

Tanya snapped, "I am tired of hearing about books you think I should read. I just want to tell you my problems."

I no longer give reading suggestions, despite feeling books are often the source of great truths. I remember a woman calling in to a radio show to say her mother opened up *Anne of Green Gables* and read a sentence or two, like some might crack open their Bible. Forever emblazed in my mind is a scene from the pages of Azar Nafisi's memoir, *Reading Lolita in Tehran,* where she sat clutching her books as if they might save her as bombs fell over her home.

During Tanya's brief visit, she planned a kayaking jaunt to see an island of seals and attended a Nia dance on the grass. She has taken vacations alone that involve yoga and chanting. I wanted to tell her to stop, sit down, take a deep breath, wait for a sign.

RICK WAS building a new vegetable bed according to *hügel-kultur*, which means "hill culture" in German. It is the ancient art of piling old logs, sticks and debris, filling in spaces with compost, leaves, and soil, and then planting seeds. As the wood slowly breaks down, naturally occurring fungi produces heat to extend the growing season. The wood traps moisture, so less watering is needed, a bonus on Gabriola where summers are dry, and our cisterns are often empty by late July. I wondered if the Germans got the idea from watching beavers build their dams.

I was contemplating this from my new spot at the Gabriola Farmers' Market, half-listening to a vendor named Barb, who had a spot next to me. She told me she has a master's degree in English literature. I think of May and wonder how she is doing, heard she moved off the island due to her husband's health.

At the market, Barb sold exotic flowers and goji berry plants in pots, along with kale and baskets of cherry tomatoes. Each Saturday her husband arrived first and set up her tent and tables and then returned with her sandwich at lunch. They were building a house up near the Legends of Spirit Rock, up on Seymour, where we once lived. It seemed like a good life the two of them were leading. I couldn't stop myself. I was jealous of anyone who had their husband home full time.

Rick had been away so much. Our yard was overrun, and there were piles of wood that needed chain sawing and a garden that needed weeding. Before he left, he had instructed me how to care for his tomatoes, his hot pepper plants, the small vining cucumbers. He had set up a confusing watering system that involved some taps being turned on; others left to drip. It was the least I could do for him, given that my arthritic knees make it difficult to move firewood or use the lawn mower or weed whacker, both of which scare me anyway.

I made organic spelt and zucchini crust pizza with halved cherry tomatoes almost every day for a week. This hardly made a dent in the herbs and vegetables growing in wild messy clumps. I made tea out of lemon balm stalks between making batches of pesto to freeze. I resented the fact that we had a garden of raised beds to feed a family of ten, and I was forced to drop off zucchini and parsley to my neighbours, Cliff

and Anne. I offered romaine to a young mother in our neighbourhood, but she never came, and I let it go to seed.

IT WAS past midnight, and I was vacuuming up stray popcorn
kernels and errant coffee beans. They rattled as they spiraled
up the long-coiled hose. I used my favourite attachment,
the pointy nozzle tool to reach under the oven. I was awake
and vacuuming at 1 AM, not because I am a clean freak, but
because I wished to communicate with my long dead mother.

Earlier this evening Tanya had called me. She told me
there was a deal, thirty dollars (US) for a half hour with her
favourite psychic, "*and* I can ask as many questions as I want."
I had always been secretly sneery about her foray into the
land of pseudoscience to help her through times of high anxiety, but this time I held my tongue.

Who am I to judge? I thought, as I yanked the wheels with
a clatter across the floor. After all the most effective salve for
a dark night of the soul, for me, is vacuuming late at night,
as the dim light of stars shine through dirty windowpanes.
People search for solace in all sorts of places, mind numbing
Netflix bingeing, boxes of wine, tubs of Ben and Jerry's—
I have tried all these things and more.

I have an old blurry photograph I took with a cheap
camera; it is of my mother, Ella, on her hands and knees, vacuuming the seat of a '70s style orange dining chair with her
FilterQueen. She is hunched over, ethereal in a midnight-blue
nightgown. Her face is smooth, she is younger than I am now,
brows furrowed, clearly not impressed that I had caught her
forever, poised, crevice tool in hand.

When she was alive, my mother kept an orderly home; no
small feat for a single mom with two children. She worked
full-time and cleaned offices on weekends. She had put my
father through university and was left without a degree. When
I think of my father, long dead now, I equate him with the

smell of smoke, from his two-pack-a-day habit. Ella banished him from our home and got to work. She planted a garden and cooked all our meals from scratch. On fall evenings, she served up minestrone soup made from her own ripe tomatoes and a dollop of fragrant basil pesto. She had a garage sale almost every weekend from June to September, selling off her father's inventory from Boston Fur Company, bulky fur coats for ten bucks each to wrinkled babas from the north end of Winnipeg.

Every afternoon, after I had walked home from Seven Oaks Elementary, I let myself in and vacuumed the entrance carpet of pine needles. My weekend chore was to do the whole house. The clunky powerhead was broken and never got repaired so I had to use the pointy crevice tool, hunched over, moving side to side like a hyena, until my neck kinked and my hand cramped.

Years later, as I vacuumed late at night, I looked around my own house. Piles of papers and library books covered every surface, but I didn't have the desire to tidy—it didn't give me the sense of Zen that vacuuming did. Instead, I plugged in my FilterQueen and ran the floor piece over the hardwood floors. I was immediately soothed by the drone of the engine. The white noise, familiar as a mother's lullaby, the click and skid of the swivel rollers, an echo from the past.

It is not lost on me that I chose to buy the same make and model that I knew as a child.

As I vacuumed, I thought about my recent decision to go back to school to get a writing degree. Last week we workshopped scripts we'd written, and I was disappointed that twice, I was cast to read the mother's roles. I shouldn't have been surprised, because after all I *was* an older woman going back to school. Although I don't feel like a mother.

Inside, I am still that same young girl that fled out west to work in the mountains after my mother's funeral. I stood, face in the wind, planting bags hanging heavy with seedlings from my hips, eager for my life of adventures to begin, unaware that one day there would be small children clinging to those same (wider) hips. Instead of hacking through piles of slash and burn, I was now wading through piles of mismatched socks, damp towels, and pet fur.

My energies would be channeled into making up play dough from scratch to amuse children while I endlessly stirred up batches of handmade soap. I cleaned mansions hauling this same FilterQueen in and out of the back of our gold Volvo. I had to find creative ways to not go mad with loneliness when Rick was away working for half the year. There were times when he was gone that I craved the presence of my mother. Some nights this yearning made me clutch my stomach in pain. But like my mother, I had to steel myself, to get things done, to not fall apart— silent sorrows swept under the rug.

I wondered is it fair that we crave our mothers while simultaneously being fearful of becoming a caricature of matronly self-sacrifice?

As I reached up to suction the pale spider web strands, I pondered how unfair it was that my mother couldn't defend herself from the small grudges that I still held in a corner of my heart. I wanted her to be home more, present more, to have time to teach me and my sister, Tanya, to make a proper pie crust or to have more than a few of memories of playing Scrabble in our kitchen on a long winter's night. I wished she had been a better role model, that she had enrolled in night courses, or went back to college, instead of searching for a new husband—another mistake.

My strongest memory is one of our last conversations. As she lay dying, instead of consoling her, I demanded that she be more than human, someone who knew all the answers to life. I have since come to understand that she was complex, fallible, human. She was a woman who vacuumed late at night, vulnerable in her bare feet and silk nightie, perhaps as an avenue to get through her own sleepless nights.

When I was thirteen, I had a dream that my mother was stuck inside the canister of the FilterQueen. In this dream, the circular walls of the vacuum were made of glass. She was trapped, knees to chin, neck at an unnatural angle. Her voice was hoarse as she talked to me through the thin walls. I instinctively knew there was nothing I could do to release her from her prison. I woke up afraid, my skin damp with sweat.

I have finally come to a place of understanding between us. Instead of remembering only the strife in our tumultuous relationship. I believe now, if she had lived longer, we might have become friends.

It was close to 2 AM, and I was in a better mood. I snickered and wondered what Mom would say if she saw me, hair disheveled, in sagging yoga pants, vacuuming with this beast of a machine with a faulty switch. Rick has repaired this machine many times and has innocently suggested we purchase a new make, a new model. I have fought him like a banshee, like he is asking me to trade in my mother.

If she were alive, she too might suggest, "Why don't you buy a Dyson?" She was nothing if not practical.

Until this clunker dies, I will continue to reach for it, when the loneliness of my long-distance marriage wells up and threatens to swallow me whole. On those nights, I will turn on the FilterQueen, the consoling vibrations offering a conduit to another place. Later, on the blurry brink of sleep, I close my eyes and see my mother—not trapped like she was in my childhood dream, but radiant, peering down from among the stars.

IN THE evenings I maneuvered our Mazda along Taylor Bay, past the never-ending ferry line-ups of work trucks, roofers, glaziers, and cabinet makers going to Nanaimo. There weren't enough workmen on Gabriola to keep up with all the new houses being built. Both tourists and islanders parked to watch sea lions wrestling fish for dinner, though most people were home by now, cooking up pots of chili or lentil stew for dinner. I unfurled myself from the car and pulled out my walking stick to make my way along the road. Some enterprising person built a tiny shack to sell art cards and driftwood mirrors.

I saw a blue heron standing still on the rocky shore. I recognized it from my nightly jaunts. It was always alone. The mountains were clear and the water was calm. A man with a permanent kink in his neck, whom I believe lives in his van, told me he saw a grey whale.

A few moments later, I heard it exhale. I looked out and saw an impressive spray of water.

It was my first-time seeing a whale here in twenty years. I watched it for a long while until bright lights and a booming intercom from the Vancouver ferry disrupted the scene.

A pair of cyclists drove by in matching gear on a tandem bike, legs in perfect harmony. Then my neighbours Cliff and Anne drove up in their pickup to enjoy the view. They used to work together on a salmon boat up in Prince Rupert. Anne told me when she first saw Cliff, she knew he was the one. Thirty-eight years later, they are still together.

The ocean glowed a pale blue and was quieter than usual. I had time to think of a documentary about beavers who mate for life. Once they pair up, they never leave each other, working together to raise their young. The males train the kits to stop up the gaps in their home with muddy plugs they carry in their tiny human-like hands.

RICK IS working in Victoria, and I have been alone for months. Chloe moved to Nanaimo to continue her education at Vancouver Island University. Stella is dead, and I miss Rick's freckled face.

Chloe and I catch the first ferry from Gabriola and head south. Chloe is visiting her boyfriend, Charlton, who is studying economics at UVic. We have to be back in Nanaimo the next morning for class. Over an hour later, and after a Starbucks, she drops me off at the government wharf at Sooke harbour, gives her dad a hug, and takes off.

Rick leads me down the steep gangplank to the twenty-two-foot dive boat, *The Seeker*. It appears too small to accommodate four people safely. It's a calm day for a ride. There is barely a whisper of a wind. The narrow boat deck is lined with empty black cages to house green urchins; full oxygen tanks are tucked below. This is the same boat Rick took me out on when we first dated. I would take the ferry over from Vancouver, buy good cheese and wine, and hole up in his motel room. It was on *The Seeker* that I felt the first lightning bolt of love.

Taylor, one of the new divers, says he got into commercial fishing because his stepfather is a diver. I ask if he wants to do anything else, but he seems content. Rick is worn out after thirty- five years so he's now the skipper, only diving when absolutely necessary.

"Let the young guys do all the hard work," he says.

I HAD hoped Rick would semi-retire as a wooden boat builder or carpenter selling furniture to Gabriola's wealthy, but he can't resist the lure of big paycheques.

Rick steers past enormous commercial fishing boats with names like *Fat Fish, Lasqueti Wrangler,* and *Adella. The Seeker* is tippy, so we balance our weight as we head to an area where the men have been working for three days. Rick plots previous dive areas electronically.

The divers are geared up before stepping onto the boat. Taylor has a muscled upper body from swimming along the bottom of the ocean raking up urchins. He stops to vape and takes a sip of water before strapping on an oxygen tank. Billy and Taylor are both in their early twenties and take turns jumping off the stern. Rick throws them each a netted bag, and they disappear under the surface. It is 8:30 AM. Rick keeps a close eye on their bubbles and watches where they pop up so he can pick them up. I remember being a dive tender in Haida Gwaii over twenty-five years ago, nervously scanning the water, waiting for Rick.

Rick cracks open the small green urchins with a metal tool like a nutcracker, scoops out a bit of roe with his dirty fingers, and places it in my mouth. The cool salty urchin melts on my tongue. When we first met, I wouldn't eat raw seafood—superfood or not.

Taylor eats standing up. Periodically a sea lion pokes its head up to investigate, and jellyfish lazily pulse by. The only sounds are the engine idling and the plonk and slosh of water on the boat's metal bottom.

A speed boat rips by with Taylor still under. Rick and Billy wave frantically to get the boat to slow down, then flip him the finger. It's both dangerous and illegal to be within a hundred metres of a working dive boat, flag flying.

We head back to the dock five hours later and tie up. The urchins are weighed by the validator, picked up by a refrigerator truck, taken to a processing plant, and flown to a market in China the next day. The life of an urchin—plucked from the ocean floor in BC to be flown across the world, and served for dinner a plane ride away.

Rick drives up in a new red Ford truck that clashes with his wild mass of orange hair. The four-hundred-pound air compressor wouldn't fit in the truck he bought two years ago, or so he says. I calculate the cost of the extra car loan and insurance and try not to panic thinking of his off season.

We go out for sushi downtown near Chinatown in Victoria. We are the only customers in the restaurant. Rick gives the sushi chef a bag filled with fresh urchin. The chef gives us a free appetizer in exchange. Rick can hardly close his hands because urchin spines have lodged in his knuckle joints. I reach out across the table, and we are the same two people who dated twenty-eight years ago.

As we sip steaming jasmine tea from tiny cups, Rick tells me how Taylor struggled against a strong tide one day when Rick was the senior diver. He used the surge of the tide to help him along.

"You can't fight it. You let it lull you," Rick says.

I have been resisting the tide. I know Rick won't stop working on dive boats. He has to work on the sea—it holds the same magic for him now as it did when he began diving thirty-five years ago and grabbed a six-gill shark or an electric stingray—who can resist touching a wild thing?

SEA URCHIN FETTUCCINE WITH BC SPOT PRAWNS

Serves 4 people

1 lb BC Spot prawns, deheaded
½ cup salted butter
2 cloves of minced garlic
½ lemon, juiced (use juice from 1 whole lemon if you like a sharp lemony flavour)
Dash of Tabasco sauce (optional, but highly recommended)
½ cup seafood or chicken broth (I often use the premade stock in tetra packs but homemade is best)
1 cup cleaned fresh sea urchin roe
Cooked pasta noodles, for serving

To prepare prawns: Place thawed headless spot prawns in boiling water. Set your timer for 3 minutes. Strain and rinse the prawns with cold water. Peel the cooked prawns and set aside until the fettucine is ready.

To make the sauce: Melt butter in a saucepan on medium heat. Add minced garlic and stir for a few minutes with a wooden spoon. Don't brown the garlic. Add the lemon juice and Tabasco sauce, then stir in the stock. Bring to a boil. Turn heat down, then add the urchin roe, and whisk this mixture. Simmer for a few minutes until it thickens.

Pour urchin sauce over pasta noodles and top with cooked BC Spot prawns. Serve with a fresh green salad and a slice of fresh sourdough bread.

EPILOGUE:
MIND THE DAYS

MY FATHER gave me a simple blank notebook as a gift, with a plain black plastic cover that says in white printed letters: Day Minder 1991. Opening the pages makes me want to sneeze. It is everything I am not—precise and orderly. It breaks down each day by a quarter hour.

I have used it to scribble notes and for a hodgepodge of recipes. It is an ancient artifact that tells the story of what our family ate, and how we entertained ourselves with complicated recipes to keep from going mad on long rainy days. Its yellowing pages include a recipe for sweet mustard with ingredients we never got. What could be more telling than a woman's handwritten cookbook before and after children?

I open it up and notice the first pages have been lost, so it starts when my new life did, when Rick and I became a couple, on the Saturday, January 5 page. I am delighted to find my trusty recipe for samosa filling from *The Moosewood Cookbook*. I see the recipe for sweet tomato and apple stovetop chutney, which was always one of my favourites. I can no longer imagine taking a whole day to prepare these dishes.

Next is cottage cheese blueberry pancakes. The page looks too clean for me to have made it, much like the handwritten recipe for avocado bean tacos.

Riffling the thin pages, I soon find my recipe for lusty curried peas, a favourite I made often when Rick and I first lived on Jamaica Road in Victoria. (This is where the killer lasagna episode took place.)

Most pages were written in blue pen, half handwriting, half printing that has grown illegible over the years. On the February 21 page is my mother's recipe for pizza dough with potato crust.

In March, there is the pickled green papaya recipe, given to me from a nurse's aide from the Philippines when I worked at Mount St. Mary Hospital. Rick loves anything strange and pickled and probably would have loved my mother's pickled pig's feet, *kholodets* in Russian.

The gnocchi recipe on March 12 is almost unreadable now. (This is the meal Hailey asked me to make before she left for her year-long trip to Australia.)

In the corner is a tiny metallic fairy sticker put there to help me find it. On March 14 is Basic Fresh Tomato Sauce with Basil for Spaghetti and Pizza. Next, I find Rick's Aunt Marie's recipe for Gingersnap Cookies that I would send as a care package to Rick up in Prince Rupert. I scan Martha Stewart's pie recipe with spiced pear and raisin filling. Its page has dark splotches and sticks to the Chocolate Zucchini Cake with Lemon Drizzle recipe, darkened with cocoa and written in red ink.

The Pizza Dough for the Bread Machine recipe I made at least once a week. It includes a cup of beer. I would use the tinny Lucky beer from a can in Rick's dive bag, which I would find rolling around between his wool socks.

PIZZA DOUGH FOR THE BREAD MACHINE

Most of my friends have tried my pizza, mainly because it has been my main go-to recipe. It is not only delicious and satisfying, it can feed a crowd. Get creative, use whatever you have hiding in the back of your refrigerator—the last handful of spinach, that half of a red onion, a jar of capers, kale, brussels sprouts, really, anything goes.

Makes 1 extra large pizza

1 cup water or beer
1 Tbsp olive oil
1 Tbsp sugar
1 tsp salt
2⅔ cups of flour
1½ tsp bread machine yeast

Optional add-ins to dough:
clove of chopped garlic,
a handful of fresh rosemary, or freshly cracked
black pepper

Preheat oven to 425°F. Put all ingredients in bread machine. (If you want to get fancy with the dough, add a clove of chopped garlic, a handful of fresh rosemary, or a grind of fresh peppercorns directly to the pizza dough before you press start.) Select dough setting.

After dough has been kneaded, pat out into a circle. Top pizza dough with ripe, sliced tomatoes; fresh basil; any combination of cheese like feta and sharp cheddar; sliced cooked sausage; raw onion slices; chopped black olives; chopped Swiss chard; parsley; or kale, and, always, always sliced pineapple. Bake for 15–20 minutes in the oven or until crust is golden brown.

My mother's husband Ronald accused people who ate pineapple on their pizzas of being gay. Mutinously, I cannot eat a pizza without pineapple chunks.

NEXT IS a recipe for eggless waffles that I used to make for
Chloe, who is allergic to everything. They were heavy as a brick.
I cooked waffles every other day, which I would serve soaked
with real maple syrup and a plunk of butter. I often snuck in a
cup of cooked butternut squash, thinking our high carb break-
fasts should be more nutritious. Tucked inside the calendar
I find an ad that was published in the *Times Colonist* news-
paper: ON-CALL MOM WORKING SHIFT WORK WOULD
LIKE TO EXCHANGE CHILDCARE. CALL 480-7085. Or:
ON-CALL MOM OF ONE INFANT, WORKING SHIFT WORK,
WOULD LIKE TO MEET THE SAME TO EXCHANGE CHILD-
CARE ON A CASUAL BASIS. I see these ads cost me $34.60.

On the page for May 28 is my morning glory muffin recipe, stuffed with carrots, one whole apple, walnuts, and whole
wheat flour. The popular blintz recipe is one I know by heart.
The Fredericton fudge recipe page is smudged with cocoa
powder. There are no recipes for salad in this book. At the
end of the book, in September, I find a play dough recipe:

PLAY DOUGH

1 cup flour   1 Tbsp cream of tartar
1 cup of water   Jell-O powder or food
1 cup of salt   colouring

Mix all ingredients except for food colouring in a medium
saucepan and cook over low heat until a solid ball forms.
Now, it's time to get creative with food coloring. Add a few
squirts of red, but not too much to make a bubble gum pink.
Or teach your kids about colour combinations and let them
assist you (supervise closely).

This recipe reminds me of the ugly buttons, dyed feathers, and tiny rolling pins in an old mandarin cardboard box that we used to store art project supplies and items needed for decorating pretend Play Dough cakes. Eventually, the Play Dough got soggy and grew mould.

ON THE December pages, there is a bubble recipe and next to it are phone numbers for child care: Rosemarie with the bad migraines; Jessica, the teenager with dark circles around her eyes whom I only used in a pinch; and Heather, blonde, friendly, and religious who had two children Hailey played with.

On Monday December 30, I wrote: "*Happy as a clam—I live in British Columbia with a heart made of wheat while Kristin works in a bakery on Granville. Like Harriet the Spy, I have found a big red guy (heart drawing) and that's no lie.*" On the next page are the words to "The Waitress Song."

At the bottom of this page it says, "*New favourite word: inkling.*" I turn the book upside down and see Rick's poorly spelled order from a Chinese restaurant: "*S & S sause, Lemmon chicken, Muchroom.*"

When Rick is feeling romantic, he makes the Caesar Salad recipe with Homemade Croutons and Fried Capers and his Easy Spicy Chicken Wings. I sip homemade Pinot Noir, nibble good cheese, and relax while he cooks. The next morning, he will hand me a latte with a dash of cinnamon, and I will do the dishes.

I can't throw this book away. It would be like burning a photo album or like giving away our family's copy of *Goodnight Moon*. I have an inkling that if it doesn't get carried off by mice, I will still have it in another twenty years. It is a relic of our past. I throw it back in the cupboard over the refrigerator, next to the African basket Marin bought me, a hand-carved mahogany bread box Rick made in boat building school, and a little box with Stella's ashes. These recipes are all written in haste, crossed out, words missing, but there was love there between the lines, so much love.

AUNT MARIE'S GINGERSNAP COOKIES

There was a time that I would make these cookies and wrap them carefully in paper towels and place them into a metal tin, sealed up tight with packing tape, and send them by mail to Rick up in Prince Rupert. I mailed them to a small store that was run by a man who would sell to fishermen. They would purchase food from him, and, in exchange, he would send along their mail and other packages. And if the fishermen and divers couldn't get to town, the men on the packer ship would pick up their food orders and mail. These care packages would reach the divers, miles away out in the ocean, in the middle of nowhere—like magic.

This was Rick's favourite cookie recipe that his Aunt Marie used to make for him. She said it is important to take away 3 Tbsp of flour in case the cookies get too dry—only add a bit more if you think the dough needs it. I taught Chloe this recipe, and her friends liked them so much, she would bring them to class at Gabriola Elementary School to share.

Makes approximately 3 dozen cookies

1¾ cups white sugar, divided

1½ cups salted butter, softened

2 eggs, beaten

½ cup cooking molasses

4 cups unbleached flour (remove 3 tablespoons of flour and add to dough a little at a time if dough looks too dry)

4 tsp baking soda

1 tsp cinnamon

1 tsp ground cloves

1 tsp ginger

½ tsp regular table salt

Cream 1½ cups of sugar and butter together with a hand-held mixer, then beat in the eggs and molasses. Mix dry ingredients together and slowly add to the wet ingredients. Grease cookie sheet.

Preheat oven to 350°F. Put remaining ¼ cup of sugar into a small bowl. Take a soup spoon and turn it upside down to dip each cookie into the bowl of sugar. Slide each spoonful of dough directly onto the prepared cookie sheet.

Gently flatten each cookie with the tines of a fork. Bake for 10–12 minutes.

ACKNOWLEDGEMENTS

I WAS INSPIRED to write this book in part because of my two babas who gave me not only love, but a love of food: oh, the perogies and all those trips to Kelekis restaurant for shoestring fries!

A huge thank you to my family and friends who helped me test and refine many of the recipes in this book including my daughters: Chloe, for helping with the lasagna so that the eggplant wasn't too soggy, and Hailey for helping with the paella. And, of course, to Rick, who whipped up gourmet meals like baked oysters or clam chowder far too many times, whenever I needed to adjust and tweak the measurements. And to everyone else who offered or shared their recipes, thank you Aunt Marie! How lucky I am, to have so many special people in my life that can cook.

I am eternally grateful for my father who instilled in me a love of words. I love words more than I love homemade gnocchi. I am also grateful for my mother who filled my childhood with art and home cooked meals. If my mother was alive, she would have been proud of me for making her blintz recipe a little bit better (by adding spelt flour).

A very special thanks to my sister, who let me write about her and our family. Bringing up the past is never easy. I truly appreciate you and love you very much. I also want to thank the rest of my family and friends who allowed me to include them in these pages.

Going back to university in my fifties was a wonderful experience. I am grateful for the support of the talented professors from Vancouver Island University's Creative Writing Department. I am especially thankful for the support of my publishing professor and friend, Joy Gugeler, whose editorial guidance, kind words, and pep talks helped propel me to the finish line.

I must also acknowledge the emotional support from many different people in my life, including my little book club, Wendy, and Emily. Having them rooting for me from the sidelines really boosted my confidence. I am also grateful for the free editing from Susan Yates. I will always value our chats about books and writing over lattes at Mad Rona's.

I would also like to thank my editor, Paula Marchese for all the thoughtful editing advice which helped bring more clarity to my story. I also appreciate her expertise with editing my recipes.

I am forever indebted to my Uncle Harvey and Auntie Laurie for taking the time to help fill in the bits and pieces of our family's past. Thank you for being supportive even if you didn't always agree on every detail.

One final note: I want to thank Rick again, not only for all the cooking but for his never-ending support, from the beginning stages when I needed a push to take that first step to learn how to write, to the times when I wasn't sure I could write at all. It was a long hard journey, but it was your patience and love that kept me going. Lucky me.

ABOUT THE AUTHOR

MARGOT FEDORUK is a writer, book reviewer and entrepreneur, whose work has been published in the *Globe and Mail*, *Quill & Quire*, BC *BookWorld*, the *British Columbia Review*, and *Portal*. She holds a BA from the University of Winnipeg and a BA from Vancouver Island University where she majored in Creative Writing. She was awarded the Barry Broadfoot Award for creative nonfiction and journalism and a Meadowlarks Award for fiction, both from VIU. She is currently working on her Masters of Library and Information Studies at the University of Alberta. For more information, visit margotfedoruk.ca.